MID-AMERICAN
★ FRONTIER ★

HISTORY

OF

THE AMANA SOCIETY

WILLIAM RUFUS PERKINS

AND

BARTHINIUS L. WICK

ARNO PRESS

A New York Times Company

New York — 1975

Editorial Supervision: ANDREA HICKS

———◆———

Reprint Edition 1975 by Arno Press Inc.

Reprinted from a copy in The State
  Historical Society of Wisconsin Library

THE MID-AMERICAN FRONTIER
ISBN for complete set: 0-405-06845-X
See last pages of this volume for titles.

Manufactured in the United States of America

———◆———

Library of Congress Cataloging in Publication Data

Perkins, William Rufus, 1847-1895.
  History of the Amana Society.

  (The Mid-American frontier)
  Reprint of the 1891 ed. published by the University, Iowa City, which was issued as no. 1 of State
University of Iowa publications, historical mono-
graphs.
  1. Amana Society. I. Wick, Barthinius Larson,
1864-   joint author. II. Title. III. Series.
IV. Series: Iowa. University. University of Iowa
publications. Historical monograph ; no. 1.
HX656.A4P4 1975   335'.9777'653   75-117
ISBN 0-405-06883-2

STATE UNIVERSITY OF IOWA PUBLICATIONS.

HISTORICAL MONOGRAPH

No. I.

HISTORY

OF

THE AMANA SOCIETY

OR

COMMUNITY OF TRUE INSPIRATION.

BY

WILLIAM RUFUS PERKINS, A.M.,

PROFESSOR OF HISTORY,

AND

BARTHINIUS L. WICK, '91.

IOWA CITY:

PUBLISHED BY THE UNIVERSITY.

1891.

PREFACE.

The account of the Amana Society, or Community of True Inspiration, which is contained in the following pages is intended to be a historical sketch of its origin and its development up to the present time. It is viewed strictly from the historical standpoint and not from the communistic. The latter phase of it has received only such attention as became necessary from its historical importance, for the full elaboration of its communistic character belongs rather to the domain of Political Science.

In order to obtain a full understanding of the true nature of the Society it has been thought necessary, and indeed it was indispensable, to enter briefly into the history of Mysticism and Pietism, the sources of its origin. This *résumé* is followed by a history of the Society from its earliest beginnings to the year 1817, illustrated by accounts of the lives of its most prominent members. Then follows a sketch of the revival of 1817, then a history of the emigration to Ebenezer, New York, and finally of that to Iowa.

Although the object of this monograph is strictly historical, brief statements have been added as to the nature of their communistic principles, their mode of life and their financial success. In the Appendixes will be found their constitution, an estimate of their property and a list of the sources and authorities consulted.

The official consent of the Society has been given to this publication, the manuscript has been read by a number of the Trustees and the statements herein contained may be considered as authoritative. This is the only paper upon the Amana Society which has received its sanction.

The Trustees have kindly given the authors access to their records and publications—the latter being intended exclusively for the use of the members and having no circulation beyond them. All of these are written and printed in the German language. From these sources have been translated the *lives* of the early members, and they have been translated without comment and with as much simplicity of diction as characterized the originals. Although it may perhaps be thought that these have been given with too much—possibly with weariness of detail, still they portray, as nothing else could portray, the tendencies which have made the Society what it is.

The authors desire to acknowledge their obligation to the Trustees of the Society for courtesy, and for aid freely given them while prosecuting their researches, and especially to thank Mr. Gottlieb Scheuner and Mr. Abraham Noé for unnumbered acts of kindness.

It is hoped that this publication, based upon exhaustive original research, and, in which sources never before consulted have been freely used, may serve to correct the many false views which prevail in this State, and in this country concerning the true character and aims of the Society.

CONTENTS.

THE AMANA SOCIETY.

The Amana Society or Community of True Inspiration, as it is called by its members, is situated in Iowa County, Iowa, about twenty miles west of Iowa City, and eleven miles east of Marengo. The Chicago, Rock Island & Pacific and the Chicago, Milwaukee & St. Paul Railways pass through or near their villages, seven in number. There are at present sixteen hundred and eighty-eight members belonging to the Society. This is what remains of that great revival movement which took place in Germany in the eighteenth century.

The story of this honest, God-fearing people is a history of suffering, of hardships and of innumerable disappointments; their piety, their uprightness and their endurance can not but command respect.

As the object of this monograph is to give a history of the Society from its *Urquelle* to the present day, it will be necessary to go back to a time anterior to its foundation and thus obtain as correct an appreciation as possible of the religious movement which took place in the latter half of the seventeenth century. This will lead us back to Mysticism and Pietism, two factors which play a conspicuous part in the church history of Germany. As the Community of True Inspiration has embodied much both of Mysticism and Pietism, we must, in order to understand the religious doctrines of the Society, trace briefly the history of these beliefs. Mysticism and Pietism are not the same, although both made a pure life essential to the attainment of future happiness.

I. MYSTICISM.

The history of Mysticism is as old as the world. It grew
into notice in Europe in the fourth century, when the followers
of Plato took for their foundation-stone his famous doctrine:
"That divine nature was diffused through all human souls;
that the faculty of reason from which proceed the health and
vigor of the mind was an emanation from God into the human
soul, and comprehended in it, the principles and elements of all
truth." These Mystics maintained that silence was the only
method by which the hidden word was excited to produce an
inward feeling of joy when the knowledge of hidden things
was shown to man. This little sect of believers spread its
doctrines towards the West. In the twelfth century they were
the most enthusiastic to expound religion; in the next century
we find the Mystics the most formidable opponents of the
Schoolmen. In the fourteenth and fifteenth centuries they
had believers all over Europe. "Up to the time of the
Reformation if any spark of real piety existed it was found
among the Mystics." [1]

After seeking God from without, they finally sought Him
from within, they listened to the 'knockings at their hearts and
had conscience judge of right and wrong.' This led to the
belief that man could come into union with God by this self-
surrender of the heart in silence to divine influence, and that
by this method could be obtained the spiritual communion
which they sought. Tholuck says, "There is a law of seasons
in the spiritual as well as in the physical world, and when the
time comes these phenomena reveal themselves in different
places."

At this period (1650-1700) Mysticism had become universal. In Spain and Italy it was named Quietism, in France it
took the name of Jansenism, in England it appeared under the
disguised name of Quakerism, and in Germany it took the
name of Pietism. In all these countries it fought against

---

[1] Dr. Howe's "*Christian History.*"

religious formality and against dogmatism; these believers put, in place of formalism, spirituality, which constitutes the highest part of man's nature. It became a religion of the heart instead of form. There was a deeply hidden cause for all this speculation. Men had become weary of the endless disputes about tenets and creeds; they had lost all faith in outward religious profession; they were at last ready to fall back on something deeper and better than mere formality; they wanted "to worship God in spirit and in truth." They claimed "God could be found by an inner light," instead of, as in the speculative age was thought necessary, by philosophic investigation. These pious believers maintained, as Schleiermacher (1768–1834) expresses it, that "religion does not reside in the intelligence or will as active powers, but in the sensibility."

In 1675 Miguel de Molinos (1627–1696), a native of Spain, but an Italian by adoption, published a book called "*The Spiritual Guide.*" It was Mystical in its nature, but it appealed to the heart and was widely read. Molinos was persecuted, and was driven from one place to another by the authorities of church and state, but his book passed from one end of Italy to the other. The religion which he tried to establish was called Quietism, for he held that 'a man to be a Christian must resign himself *quietly* to God.' Molinos maintained that man needed no mediator between himself and God, but that every man could seek Christ without any human help, and be forgiven. This bold doctrine was too much for that age, and the brave Molinos was put into prison. His only crime was that he preferred the religion of the heart to that of the rosary; he wanted to do away with superstitious formality and put in place of it a religious devotion in which all could take part. As he would not retract what he felt to be the truth, he was placed in close confinement until his death, probably in 1696.

The work of Molinos was taken up in France by that admirable woman, Madame Guyon (1648–1717), a woman of deep and sincere piety. Her books are full of spiritual thought, of practical charity and disinterested love. She commands "prayer in silence, prayer unlimited to times or seasons, unhindered by words." She calls this condition "a state of feeling rather than an act, a sentiment rather than a request, a continued sense of submission, which breathes moment by moment from the serene depths of the soul." In her efforts to promote true Christianity she was assisted by Fénelon, the great prelate, who eloquently supported the doctrine of Quietism. That such a great man should defend Mysticism set the ecclesiastical authorities to thinking. The end of the long controversy that followed was that Madame Guyon was ordered to retire to Switzerland, and Fénelon was severely denounced by the authorities of the church and banished from court. Although Mysticism had many other advocates, with the loss of these two the influence of the tidal wave of Mysticism which was sweeping over Europe at this time, ceased in France.

Vaughan says: "In France we have the mysticism of sentiment, in Germany the mysticism of thought." A great many of the German Mystics have been secluded students; such, at least, was Thomas à Kempis. He perhaps had more influence than any of the rest, for he leaves out philosophy and intellect and appeals to the heart. The works of Kempis have been read by thousands of people. He is simple and plain and can be easily understood by the uneducated. Tauler is another, who turned away from the schools to intuitionism, saying that "religion is something that can not be revealed by any method of human wisdom, but is revealed direct from God."

The most noted Mystic of Germany, however, was Jacob Böhme (1575–1624), a poor shoemaker of Silesia. In his soul there was a deep consciousness of right and wrong; he felt that he was inspired by an inward light which taught him the essence of all things. Böhme accomplished a great work for the church in Germany, for he summoned the people to awake from their lethargy and examine their hearts. His works are many. The "*Aurora*" is the best known. Schlegel says that "Böhme is equal, if not superior, to Klopstock, Milton, and

Dante." A recent writer has said that he could not see how so great a doctrine (the inward light) could have originated in so ignorant a man. It is true that Böhme was not educated in the schools—neither was Shakespeare, for that matter—but Böhme was a born philosopher, whose writings have been studied by such men as Hegel, Schelling, and Kant. He has still many followers in Germany. The writings of Böhme were widely read throughout Germany. Johann Arndt (1555-1621), a minister of much enthusiasm, was very much impressed with Böhme's doctrine of "inward light." He wrote a book called "*True Christianity*," which at once acquired celebrity and has since become a standard work among all religious denominations. John Gerhard followed in the footsteps of Arndt. His "*Exegetical Explanation of Particular Passages*" produced a great excitement, for he advocated the doctrine of Inspiration with such vehemence and enthusiasm that the people could not but believe. Another of Böhme's school is John Valentin Andreæ. He wrote a satire[1] on the times which set Germany on fire. The clergy condemned the work as spurious, and branded the author as an enemy of the church, but the denunciations of the clergy did no harm; a reaction set in and opinion changed, for the book had exposed the dry formalism and the sectarian strife of the times. It was a work which denounced the shams which had crept into the Lutheran and Reformed churches; it demanded new life, called boldly for reinvigoration, and this came in the form of Pietism, which had risen from the seed sown by the early Mystics.

II. PIETISM AND ITS MISSION.

Pietism is a word used in church history in the latter half of the seventeenth century, and applied to the belief of a party of German Lutherans who were dissatisfied with the cold formalism of the clergy. They did not separate from the

---

[1] *The Discovery of the Brotherhood of the Honorable Order of the Holy Cross.*

church, but held their own meetings in private houses. These meetings were called "Collegia Pietatis," from which we have the name Pietist.

The founder of this sect was Philip Jacob Spener, an eminent Lutheran divine, who began these meetings in his own house at Frankfort, about 1670. Spener was born in Elsass, 1635, and died at Berlin, 1705. He was one of the most remarkable men in the Lutheran church. From early childhood he was reared amid pious surroundings, and from youth up he was possessed of a serious and retired disposition. When a mere child he read Arndt's "*True Christianity*," which made such a deep impression on his mind that he even then took a vow to serve the church faithfully and to further Christ's kingdom here on earth,—a vow to which he ever remained faithful. He completed his education at Strasburg, and for three years he attended several of the higher institutions of learning in Germany. He was for a short time a minister in Strasburg. He removed from that city to Frankfort-on-the-Main, where he began his work of reform. Here, he soon gathered around him a large multitude of earnest seekers after truth. The clergy of the church spent all their time in disputes over doctrinal points, and left their flocks to take care of themselves. Spener cared little for doctrine, for he based religion on truth and the Bible. He discarded the high-flown language then in use,— an affectation which had crept in—and used a simple, clear style, which the common people could understand. But he found this was not enough, so he organized weekly meetings at his house, where all were allowed to speak. These meetings were the small beginnings of the great movement which took place in the Lutheran church. In 1675, Spener published his great work, "*Pia Desideria.*" In this book he shows what is needed in the church, to make it once more as effective as in the time of Luther. He maintains in this book that "the word of *God* should be spoken, and not learned discourses on other subjects, such as philosophy and science; pious people of all classes should act as ministers if capable; love and piety are neces-

sary for all preachers, in order that they may urge others
to see the importance of faith and its fruits." This book was
approved by the church, but it was severely criticised by the
clergy, whose faults he denounced in strong terms. Spener
laid much stress upon the necessity of a new birth. He said
that bread and wine did not help a man if there were not a
change of heart; that all amusements should be prohibited;
that the mode of dress should be for comfort and not for
style. He urged the common people to read the Scriptures
daily at their homes, and to attend meetings of worship during the week. All philosophy and book-learning he despised,
for it came not from the heart, and it could not satisfy the
yearning soul who sought for truth. Spener may have been
too enthusiastic for his cause, which he felt was right, but such
a fearless, brave man was needed to gather together the pious
followers of Böhme, Arndt and Andreæ. Dorner, the his-
torian, says that "this awakening was necessary in the development of Protestanism." Another author says that "Pietism
went back from the cold faith of the seventeenth century to
the living faith of the Reformation." Something had to be
done to arouse the church from its lethargy.

As a remedy the following means of improvement were
proposed by the Pietists:—

I. That the scholastic theology which reigned in the
academies, and was composed of intricate and disputable
doctrines and obscure and unusual forms of expression, should
be totally abolished.

II. That polemical divinity, which comprehended the con-
troversies subsisting between Christians of different com-
munions, should be less eagerly studied and less frequently
treated, though not entirely neglected.

III. That all mixture of philosophy and human science
with divine wisdom was to be most carefully avoided; that is,
that pagan philosophy and classical learning should be kept
distinct from, and by no means should supersede Biblical
theology.

IV. That, on the contrary, all students who were intended

for the ministry should be kept accustomed from their youth up, to the perusal and study of the Holy Scriptures, and be taught a plain system of theology drawn from these unerring sources of truth.

V. That the whole course of their education should be so directed as to render them useful in life, by the practical power of their doctrine, and the commanding influence of their example.[1]

These articles were just what the church needed, but through jealousy and internal strife they were never adopted into the church creed. This was a great mistake, for although a great many of the Pietists remained in the church, they gave up the work they had begun, at the time of Spener's death. Many joined other denominations, some founded new sects, and still others took up Rationalism as the last resort. If the church had possessed more spirit and less dogmatic indifference, the pious followers of Spener, full of enthusiasm for their cause, would have swelled the numbers of the Lutheran church, and they would have stood firm and fast against the Rationalistic doctrines which took root in German soil about this time; but, as it was, these believers, becoming disgusted with the dogmatic strictness of the church, left it.

After the Pietism of Spener had somewhat died out, the Lutheran church fell back to what it was, when Spener took up the reform movement in 1670. There were still pious believers, but they were put under the ban of the church or exiled from their native land. "Thus these outcasts from the church, driven away from their native land, were now like sheep without a shepherd. But God in His mercy caused a spiritual wind to blow, soothed the troubled souls in their afflictions, and raised up in their midst persons who were inspired."[2] These persons assembled for worship in private houses, as the Pietists had done. In these meetings many seemed to be inspired, and told many things which were to happen in the future. Thus arose at several places in Ger-

---

[1] Watson, "*Theological Dictionary*," Art. Protestant Pietism.

[2] *Inspirations Historie*, I., von Gottlieb Scheuner, pp. 8–9.

many many who prophesied like the prophets of old. These people were called Inspirationists.

The first one who fell into fits of ecstasy and prophesied that God would raise up a new sect, was a lady of noble rank, by the name of Rosamunde Juliane, of Asseburg. From 1679–1686 she became inspired five times. She was of a religious turn of mind, and spent much of her time in prayer. She began to see sights, fell into raptures, and then began to prophesy. This woman became the laughing-stock of the neighborhood; she was persecuted and driven out of town, but still she clung to her religious principles. Dr. Johann W. Petersen, a learned professor of Lüneburg, a worthy follower of Johann Arndt, and a man well versed in theology and grounded in the Lutheran faith, became interested in this pious, simple-hearted woman. He visited her while in prison, and they conversed on religion in general, and especially on the doctrine of Inspiration as she understood it. Petersen became convinced that Inspiration could as well take place now as in the time of the prophets. He defended openly the testimony of this woman, and in return was ridiculed and mocked by the clergy, who looked upon her as a simple-hearted enthusiast. Petersen lost his position as professor, and was driven out of town by the enraged rabble.

From 1693–1700 he travelled, and became subject to Inspiration many times. While under this influence he saw much which was to take place in the church. He saw that a new sect would originate, different from all others. It would go back to the time of the apostles for doctrines, and would follow the Scriptures.[1] Many of these visions he wrote down and had printed for private circulation: Others soon joined Petersen, whose amiable disposition and exemplary life helped to win many friends. In 1700 a poor cooper, by the name of Myer, began to prophesy, saying that "God would raise up a man who should take care of the faithful little flock that wandered throughout Germany without a shepherd.[2]

---

1 See "*Works*" of Johann W. Petersen.

2 See *Inspirations Historie*, I., p. 9.

The first ones who tried to form a new sect of those who believed in Inspiration were three brothers from Halberstadt, in Saxony. Their names were Johann Tobias, Johann Heinrich, and August Friedrich Pott. The latter had studied theology at Halle, and was a warm admirer of the illustrious Francke. From 1708–1712 they travelled much in search of pious believers, and religious Mystics. They finally settled down at Hanau, where a new sect called the " *Wieder-taüfer* " (Anabaptists) had sprung up, led by Alexander Mack. Many of Mack's followers joined the Pott brothers, and in Ysenburg a few pious people left the established church and came to Hanau. A woman of high rank, Eva Catherina Wagnerin, from Ronneburg, became so enraptured with the doctrine of Inspiration, which the Pott brothers advocated, that she also joined the little congregation, in which she took an active part as a minister of the gospel.

These were the small beginnings of those mystical doctrines which were formulated and improved by Eberhard Ludwig Gruber and Johann Friedrich Rock, who are looked upon as the real founders of the Society. It is around these two men, their "heroes of faith," that the development and progress of the Community has turned as if on an axis. They were both from Würtemberg. The former was a clergyman in the Lutheran church, but lost his position because he defended the doctrines of Spener, and because he tried to do away with the outward forms of religion, which are always magnified more when the spirit of true religion dies out; and put in place of them the religion of the heart, such as Spener had advocated. For this, Gruber had to withdraw from the church. Rock was a preacher's son, of a peculiar temperament and of a mystical cast of mind. He was a saddler by trade, but had received a good education He read much about religion, but found no sect whose doctrines could satisfy his yearnings after truth. In Stuttgart he found a small body of serious believers presided over by a Dr. Hedinger. It was at one of Hedinger's meetings that Gruber and Rock met for the first time; an intimate friendship arose between them, which lasted for life.

After Hedinger's death this little flock of believers was scattered. Gruber and Rock removed to Himbach where they could enjoy more religious freedom. Here they lived secluded and alone from 1707–1714, reading and meditating on the mysteries of religion. On the 16th of November, 1714, John T. Pott and Gottfried Neumann, who had heard of Gruber and Rock, came to visit them. The same evening a public meeting was held. It is from this meeting that the Society dates its origin. A little band composed of E. L. Gruber, his son Johann Adam Gruber, J. F. Rock, Johann T. Pott, Johanna Melchior and G. Neumann, were the first ones to join together in Christian fellowship for the organization of a new sect, based not upon any code of external sanctity, but based upon truth and a belief that God could now as of old, inspire chosen prophets who should act as messengers to men. These ministers went about preaching, so that in a short time the Society had many adherents. Gruber and Rock were the most influential in preaching, and around these two men the obscure and the illiterate assembled to hear explained and unfolded the principles of that spiritual kingdom which all sought to find. Patiently and assiduously Rock and Gruber labored to instruct their countrymen in divine things and in the knowledge of virtue. These men wanted to free the ignorant peasants from the heavy burdens imposed by the corrupt clergy, and to lead them to a purer and more exalted communion with God. To accomplish this end they toiled and suffered all sorts of persecution; firm in their belief they unostentatiously went into every nook and corner of Germany, penetrated into Switzerland, and visited many parts of France and Holland. The gentleness of their manners, the purity and simplicity of the doctrines they preached, convinced many, but the hatred of the clergy, who looked with disgust on any change in the form of things, knew no bounds. The preachers were put in prison, they were fined and persecuted, but they were not silenced.

The difference between the Community organized by Gruber and Rock and many of the other Inspiration communities throughout Germany and Holland, was that the former maintained that there was false as well as true Inspiration. Very frequently in the history of the Society we find Inspirationists whom the Society condemned as false. This gift of Inspiration continued in a person for a time, and then departed. Johann Schwanfelder, a member of the Society, was inspired for only three months. The Pott brothers, who made such a glorious beginning in the Society, ceased also to speak by the end of 1714.

In 1715 Ursula Mayerin came from Switzerland to visit the members of the Society. She became convinced and began to preach. As she was a woman of good understanding and of a pious disposition, she exercised a great influence over the people with whom she came in contact.

As the Society increased in membership, persecution began. The two Grubers, father and son, were driven out of Marienborn, where they had conducted meetings. In their struggle to maintain free worship, guided, as they thought, by an inward light, these heroic men walked bravely from city to city, proclaiming the word of God in church, town hall, or on the streets. Kessler and Strahl, two ministers of the Lutheran church in Zweibruck, joined them.

The common people, who could not understand how these ministers could talk by Inspiration, said that they were possessed of the devil. The faculty at Halle, where Pietism had taken the deepest root under the illustrious Francke, now turned a cold side to the Society which tried to perpetuate those doctrines. A few members of the faculty wrote long pamphlets trying to disprove the doctrines of Inspiration, saying that if it really existed it could come from no other source than from the Evil Spirit.[1] These accusations did not retard the growth of the Society, but rather had the opposite effect, since by these means the doctrines were spread so much more.

Many of these members were perhaps over-zealous in the cause for which they labored, for at times they felt it was

---

[1] *Inspirations Historie*, I., p. 19.

right to preach before kings,[1] prophesying many things which
were to take place. Very often they appeared before the
magistrates, saying, the wrath of God would come on those
who did not cease persecution; at other times they went into
the churches when the clergymen were conducting services.
When Inspiration came, these men would stand up and begin
to speak, soon drowning the clergyman's voice, and having
the entire congregation as listeners. J. A. Gruber prophesied
in Gelnhausen, 1715, that the clergyman of that place would
die suddenly. The clergyman caused Gruber to be arrested.
He lingered in prison for several months, being denied a trial.
Finally he was taken out of town by the officers, who told
him never to return. A few days after Gruber was taken
from jail the clergyman whom Gruber had mentioned did die
suddenly.[2]

In Holland many began to prophesy like the members of
the Society of True Inspiration, but those were looked upon
as possessed by false inspiration.

In the Society of True Inspiration, a committee was always
appointed to examine those who spoke by Inspiration, to find
out whether they really were inspired, or if they only believed
they were. In the history of the Society there were many
who were denied the privilege of prophesying.

In October, 1715, the third love feast was held. These
feasts were held, not at any stated time or place, but when it
was thought desirable for the strengthening of the members,
or when new converts were made, and when their ministers
were released from prison. There was generally a week's
preparation, when the members were tested by the elders to
see if they were prepared. If the members were not in a
spiritual mood they could not take part. After this examination, a day was spent in prayer, when they had feet-washing,
and finally the love feast. This religious festival is held
quarterly now by the Moravians and Methodists, in imitation

1 The rulers of the petty states of Germany were often called kings.
2 See *Inspirations Historie*, l., p. 24.

of the *Agapæ* held by the early Christians, at the time of the communion, when contributions were made for the poor.

Johann Carl Gleim, a minister of the Society, while staying in an inn over night, fell in with a great number of gamblers and drunkards. As he sat in his room quietly engaged in prayer, the power of the spirit arose in him, and he went down and addressed them, saying if "they did not repent God would surely send visitations upon them." In less than a year great floods occurred, in which many of these persons lost their lives.[1]

In 1717 Johann Adam Gruber and H. S. Gleim went into a church at Zürich and preached to the people. This bold step so enraged the clergyman, who feared that the members would leave the church in which he labored, and go over to the Inspirationists, that he caused them to be arrested. The following was the sentence:—

"Since J. A. Gruber, from Würtemberg, and H. S. Gleim, from Hessen, have held meetings in this town, of a religious nature, and since they have distributed pamphlets praising their own Society and degrading our church, therefore has this council decided by a majority vote that (1) their pamphlets shall be burned publicly by the executioner; (2) that said persons be put in the pillory; (3) that they be lashed through the principal streets; (4) that hereafter said persons be forbidden to enter this land."[2]

They were first put in the pillory, where they were exposed to the cutting comments of the mob. They were then driven through the streets, each prisoner receiving sixty-two lashes; the blood from their backs ran down the streets of Zürich, but still the stern clergy and thousands of spectators followed the procession, and cheered in derision whenever the prisoners groaned from the pain inflicted by the lash. Such proceedings sound like those of the Inquisition, but this was done in enlightened Germany and permitted by the Lutheran church. Two years afterwards H. S. Gleim died at Schwarzenau, his

---

1 *Inspirations Historie*, I., p. 65.
2 *Inspirations Historie*, Vol. 2, p. 123.

death due no doubt to the hard treatment he had experienced in prison.

In 1718 Johann A. Gruber went to America and settled at Germantown, Pennsylvania. He kept up constant communication with the Society, and once returned to see his aged father, but never founded any branch of the Society in America. A descendant of J. A. Gruber was an active member in the Methodist church in the beginning of this century. J. C. Gleim, a brother of the former, and B. D. Mackinet joined Gruber in America. The communication kept up from both sides of the water undoubtedly brought the members in Germany to think about America as a "promised land," though emigration did not take place until 1844, over a century later.

Up to 1720 the work had been mostly done by travelling ministers; they really had no organization, nor did they have any set meetings for worship. In this year an organization was made with Gruber and Rock as presiding elders; meetings were established at Schwarzenau, Himbach, Frankfort, Ronneburg, and Birstein, nearly all of which are in Hessen. It is in this principality that most of the members lived, and to which many came from Switzerland, Bavaria, and Elsass, since there was more religious freedom given in Hessen than in any of the other states in Germany. At that time each little state had its own laws and government.

Rock and Gruber often prophesied about events which would take place. Thus, for example, Rock said in 1718 that Frankfort would be laid in ashes, which actually took place the next year. At Halle, Rock found the Pott brothers living in retirement, still believing in the Society, but they had lost the gift of Inspiration. In 1720 Rock and J. J. Schulthes visited Switzerland, where a large number of pious people joined the Society.

Casper Löw of Nürnberg, a firm believer and a pious, God-fearing man, handed an epistle to the Burgomaster, begging him to be more lenient to the seekers after truth. For this offence Löw and Rock were put in the stocks, to be ridiculed and mocked by the citizens.

As the members were scattered they were unable to attend meetings. A great many moved from distant places to Himbach, where a large congregation was gathered together. Himbach from this time on became the principal headquarters of the Society.

In Tübingen, where the clergy were very immoral, one of these ministers of the Society felt it his duty to walk into one of the principal churches and lay a testimonial on the altar.[1] It was a plea for more true Christianity within the church. This displeased the clergy, who were greatly excited about the matter, and the poor exposer of wrongs, and believer in the purification of religion was arrested.

J. P. Arnoldi, of Frankfort, was imprisoned in 1726, because he had said in a meeting that "God's curse would surely come upon the city on account of the people's sins."[2]

More and more of the Swiss joined the Society which now had established meetings at Zürich, Bern, Schaffhausen, and Welschen-Schweiz.

In 1728 Johann A. Gruber returned from America to see his aged father before he died. This old man, who had worked hard to collect the little flock of Pietists, was now about to leave them forever. He died, December 11, 1728, at sixty-three years of age. Gruber was born in Stuttgart; he was sent to school at an early age, where he was quick and proficient. From Stuttgart he was sent to Tübingen, in Würtemberg. After graduating he began preaching, in which field he soon became noted outside his parish. He was both an orator and a logical thinker; and the amiability of his disposition and the uprightness of his character no doubt won for him friends and admirers. A firm believer in the doctrine of Spener, and aware of the immoralities of the clergy, Gruber did not shrink from what he called his duty—that was, to denounce the immoralities which had crept into the church,—in the severest terms. He said: "Since the clergy should be examples for the people, they

---

[1] *Inspirations Historie*, I., p. 131.
[2] *Inspirations Historie*, I., p. 135.

ought to practice what they preached." He became acquainted with Dr. Hedinger, an eminent divine, famous throughout Würtemberg for his eloquence in defending true Christianity and maintaining that "faith was not enough in man—there must be associated with faith, works." Hedinger and Gruber worked together until the former's death, in 1707. Gruber also became acquainted with Wilhelm Petersen, formerly mentioned, and Dr. Carl, a man of learning and much piety. These men had a great influence over Gruber, who was a seeker after truth. Gruber was of a nervous, excitable temperament. At times he felt that he could prophesy, but he attributed this feeling to his peculiar temperament. In the meantime he wrote much against Inspiration, a wave of which was at this time sweeping over Germany. Finally J. F. Rock, Gruber's friend, began also to have the same peculiar feelings that Gruber had felt for several years. Johann Adam Gruber, the son, began to show signs of inward emotions. In 1714, when the Pott brothers came to visit him, Gruber changed his mind and became convinced that Inspiration was true, that the feelings which had been working in his mind during those years, and which he had never given time to mature, were truly from God. As formerly he had written zealously against Inspiration, he now with equal fervor defended it in a large book on false and true Inspiration, published in 1715. In the same year he published his twenty-one rules which the Society adopted as its creed.[1] Gruber is also the author of many hymns which are full of love for men.

In the death of Gruber the Society lost its greatest leader, a loss which was never made good. It was Gruber who first collected the little body of believers, who formulated the doctrines of their creed, and who spread those doctrines beyond the boundaries of Germany.

J. F. Kessler was appointed elder, in place of Gruber, at Schwarzenau. Kessler had been a minister in the Reformed church, and joined the Society of True Inspiration some years earlier.

---

[1] For the twenty one rules see "*Life of Gruber.*"

In 1730, Count Nicholas L. von Zinsendorf, of the Herrnhüt Society, in Saxony, visited the society at Schwarzenau. The Herrnhüt Society was a remnant of the Bohemian Brothers, who had remained secluded in Moravia. In 1722 a few of these brethren escaped to Saxony and settled on the lands of Count Zinsendorf, where they built a castle called Herrnhüt (The Keep of God). Count Zinsendorf became their leader, and as he was well educated and of noble birth, he exercised a great influence on the later history of the Society, which now exists around the world.

It is distinguished for its zeal in the mission field. There are at present 15,000 members in Europe, and 7000 in the United States. The Moravians, or, as they are sometimes called, United Brethren, live in distinct communities, unite their interests very closely, but do not hold a community of goods. They hold meetings on Sunday, when sermons are delivered and the church creed is read. Music takes a prominent part in their worship.[1] They were firm believers in the doctrine of Spener, and hold much in common with the community of True Inspiration.

The visit of Zinsendorf to Schwarzenau brought about a friendly intercourse between the two societies. Both denominations believed they were moved by the same spirit; both sought to serve God in a more rigorous manner than other denominations. On leaving, Zinsendorf spoke as follows: "We see plainly that God's grace works powerfully among you, as among us. With us the work takes place in the church, with you out of the church. Each one works where God placed him. No one of us shall hinder you in your work, but we give you our hand as a mark of friendship, that we may work in peace side by side for the cause of God."[2]

Some discussion arose between the two societies concerning Inspiration, but perfect harmony always existed   Some of

---

[1] For information concerning this society, see "*Works of Count Zinsendorf;*" also "*Moravian Brothers,*" and others.

[2] *Inspirations Historie,* I., p. 161.

the Society of True Inspiration joined the Moravians, while a nephew of Zinsendorf and several Moravians joined the Society. Both societies worked for, and aimed at, one end; viz., how to make people purer and better. Amid all the vicissitudes of life members of both of these societies have shown an undaunted courage, an ardent zeal, and a sincere love for their fellowmen.

In 1733, a person joined the Society of True Inspiration who took an active part in spreading the doctrines that Gruber had defended so eloquently. This was Jonas Wickmark, a Swede, who, after graduating from the university of his native land, had gone to Jena, where he took a course in law, in order to fully equip himself for his chosen profession, which he intended to practice on his return home. While at Jena, Wickmark had studied and thought much concerning Pietism, and before leaving Germany he wanted to see the Society which had adopted so many of Spener's doctrines. On this visit he felt so comforted with the simple faith which these people practiced that he gave up his journey home, where office and honors awaited him, for a life among these pious people. He was well versed in the languages and wrote short-hand, which he used in taking down sermons, which were preserved and printed for distribution. He was never Inspired, but often spoke in their meetings, and travelled much in Holland, Elsass and Switzerland, in company with J. F. Rock. Wickmark wrote much in defense of the Society, and many beautiful hymns come from his pen. He looked after the little flock not only in spiritual, but in temporal affairs as well. He died in 1786, at the advanced age of 87, having worked faithfully in the Society for fifty-three years; and in all that time he never visited his native land.

Another prominent man in the Society was Johann Georg Metz, from Elsass, who joined the Society in 1716, after he was exiled. Metz was the great-grandfather of Christian Metz, who died in 1867, the most noted worker on this side of the Atlantic.

Frau von Stein, a lady of noble birth, well educated, reared in wealth and luxury, became tired of the hollowness of fashionable society, in which she could find nothing that satisfied her longings for truth.   She retired from the ball room to her closet, where she spent much of her time in prayer and in reading religious books.   Having heard much about the Society, and wishing to know more, she was visited by several of the members.   She was so impressed with the simplicity of their religion and the plainness of their manners, that she became fully convinced of the truth of their doctrines, and joined the Society, in which she took an active part.

The elders, and many of those who spoke through Inspiration, travelled much, continually organizing new meetings and preaching the gospel wherever they went.   They put on trial those who claimed that they spoke through Inspiration, tested all the members, and openly reprimanded them.   Preachers in the Established Church and the magistrates were also warned that if they did not turn from their evil ways, they would surely be punished by a just God.   For such bold utterances they were lashed at the whipping-post, scorned by the people, and often put in prison, where they lingered for months without trial.   Such severe treatment only strengthened their belief, made them more enthusiastic in their cause, and more willing to suffer for the sake of conscience.

Paul G. Nagel, the son of an attorney in Würtemberg, a graduate of the University of Jena, joined the Society in 1740. He was an attorney by profession, and a man of much learning, who became useful to the Society in many ways.   At Rock's death, in 1749, Nagel became elder in his place, an office which he filled to the satisfaction of all.

Johann F. Rock died in 1749, aged seventy years.   Rock was an able man, in fact one of the pillars of the Society. Having a strong constitution, he travelled much as a minister, and was very often imprisoned for his bold utterances of truth.   He suffered untold hardships, sleeping on a little straw or on the bare, stone floor in damp jails, without fire and without much food.   He spent the last thirty-five years of his life, constantly travelling either alone or in company with his faithful companion, Jonas Wickmark, who took Rock's sermons down in shorthand, and had many of them printed and distributed after Rock's death. Rock was of a lively temperament, earnest and enthusiastic for social reform, which had reached a low ebb during the reigns of Frederick William I., and Frederick II. As a minister, Rock was fluent, persuasive, and eloquent. Endowed with much sympathy for his fellowmen, he worked on their feelings and reached their hearts. He cared little for priest or magistrate, if he knew they were immoral, and did not properly fill the offices for which they were chosen. He was accustomed to speak in all places,—on the streets, in the fields, in the inns, and in the churches,—wherever he could find a place. People turned out to hear him in all places; nowhere was he without hearers, for all wanted to see the man who cared to flatter none, and to serve none but his God. Gruber may have been a deeper thinker, but Rock was a more fluent speaker. Both were enthusiastic in the cause they represented. The former, formulated the doctrines with his pen, the latter spread those doctrines in person throughout all Germany, Holland and Switzerland. Gruber was a student of a retired disposition, while Rock had been a man of the world, and loved to mingle with men; both were necessary to the Society, for the one laid down the principles of their creed, while the other expounded and explained those principles to the people. Both maintained that man was not saved by faith alone, but that good works were necessary. They laid great stress on virtue. Honesty, uprightness, morality, were strictly enforced on members of the Society. These men emphasized the fact that there must be ethics in government, in politics, in religions,—a problem that the nineteenth century has tried to solve. Social as well as religious reform these men sought to accomplish, and this is the reason such an outcry arose from the mass of the people, who did not want to be disturbed in the practice of their old customs. Although these persons did not convert all Germany, they did arouse public sentiment, both in church and in state, so that the reform movement they began has since become a reality.

Rock was the son of a preacher, of a wild disposition and a lover of games. He wandered about after receiving his education, without any settled profession. He was a saddler by trade. He lived in Berlin, in Strasburg, and at Halle, at which places he spent much of his time in reading. While perusing the pages of a book one disagreeable Sunday afternoon,[1] disgusted with life and the hollowness of the society in which he moved, he took a solemn vow to change his mode of life, a vow which never was broken, for he remained faithful to the end. He now tried to find a sect which he could join. At one time he contemplated joining the Socinians. In this manner he passed much time in reading and meditation. After six years wandering Rock returned to his mother, who was now a widow and lived at Stuttgart. His mother in the meantime had joined a body of pious people, who met in private houses for silent worship. Rock, who had meditated much on religion, joined this little company. The members increased in number, until the clergy became frightened, for the believers went to the silent meetings instead of coming to church to listen to soulless sermons, to philosophic discussions which had puzzled Plato and Aristotle. The clergy, influential among the princes and the magistrates, caused a law to be passed, 1707, that all who did not attend church should be compelled to leave the city.[2] Rather than disobey the dictates of conscience, Rock, his mother, and younger brother, with many others, left their comfortable homes, their friends and their all, to become exiles and outcasts, not knowing where to turn their course, fearing to be driven still further in their flight in search of freedom for religious belief. This, in the land where Luther and Melancthon had accomplished so much for the Freedom of thought! After wandering around for some time in search of a new home, they finally settled down in Ysenburg, a district of Hessen. Here they found E. L. Gruber, who also had fled from Stuttgart. In the fall of 1714, the Pott brothers before

---

[1] See "*Autobiography of J. F. Rock.*"
[2] See "*Autobiography of J. F. Rock.*"

mentioned, and Johanna M. Melchior held a meeting at Gruber's house. Rock was invited, and as he entered the house Johanna M. Melchior was in Inspiration and spoke of unbelief. When she ceased speaking, the younger Pott also fell into a sort of trance, and began to speak in the same strain. Rock felt that the words went to his heart. He thought it was the beginning of a new religion,—a religion which he formed and remodelled. Rock soon began to experience similar feelings, and became inspired in meeting. One day while at work in the garden, he felt that he must leave his work and go to two pious old people, and tell them to prepare for death, for one of them would soon die. He went to see them, delivered his message, but could not understand it, for they were both in perfect health. In less than a week one of them died.[1]

At other times Rock had the feeling that he must go before kings, magistrates and ministers, to tell them to be more lenient in their laws and more godly in their lives, or else God would punish them.[2] In the night he could not sleep, but wandered around in the fields, shedding tears over the evil life he had led, praying for forgiveness for his sins.

After a long season of repentance and prayer, Rock started out to preach. In Tübingen he attended church, and, when exercises were over, walked up to the altar and begged to be permitted to deliver a sermon on penitence. This act so enraged the clergyman that he marched Rock down to the city hall, had him arrested, and burned the papers found on his person. In his autobiography are found many interesting stories gathered from the travels which he made up to the time of his death. These stories give us a good idea of the age in which he lived, and of the character of the people. Rock was popular with the people and was highly respected. He knew how to touch the right chord in his hearers, and he could always impress his own personality on the congregation. His character was above reproach, and his zeal for the cause

1 See his "*Autobiography*."
2 See his "*Autobiography*."

of true religion was as fervent as had been the yearnings of
his own soul in search of truth.

From the death of Rock to the revival in 1817, the Society
was declining. The reason for this is doubtless due to the
fact that the great work which Gruber and Rock had taken
up was left to men who did not possess the power, or the
personality that the founders were endowed with. Perhaps
the incessant wars of Frederick the Great had also something
to do with the prosperity of the Society, for in a war for
existence, like the "Seven Years' War," where the integrity
of the country was at stake, the thoughts, the actions, the
very existence of the people depend on victory. Another
reason for the decline of the Society was that religious thought
had nearly disappeared, and Rationalism held complete sway
over the mass of people, its influence increased by the
king's indifference to religion, and Voltaire's stay in Germany.
The universities adopted this fashionable mode of thinking.
The students were in ecstacy over the writings of Lessing,
who, from 1750 to the time of his death, 1781, exercised a
great influence not only on literature, but on religious thought,
— an influence tending toward Rationalism. These causes
affected religious thought as a whole. The Lutheran, the
Reformed, the Catholic churches, all suffered from this wave
of Rationalism. It was the foreboding of the French Revolution. The Society of True Inspiration suffered with the
rest, and, with the loss of its leaders, it seemed at one time that
it was about to be hurled into the maelstrom created by the
waves which were forming and threatening from France; but
it lived on and survived the Revolution, when new life was
breathed into it by the revival movement in the beginning of
this century.

From the organization of the Society, the members had objected to oaths and wars. As they felt it to be a duty of conscience they objected to take an oath, but declared themselves
willing to make an affirmation equally strong. For this, they
were accused of disloyalty to the state, and called traitors to
religion, and haters of truth. They were thrown into prison,

tortured, and publicly whipped, but they maintained the same stoical perseverance in the cause of truth that the early Christians had shown under the Roman Empire. The custom of the oath which these people so firmly opposed, and thought to be inconsistent with the Scripture teachings, has now in a great measure been superseded by affirmation.

In the continuous wars of Frederick the Great, all Prussia was under arms. As the members refused to go to war, they were persecuted in all ways imaginable. Some lingered in prison, others were compelled to bear arms, and still others either died from ill treatment, or were actually put to death. In spite of such cruel treatment, they maintained their ground, willing to meet death rather than sully themselves with what they thought to be an atrocious sin, viz: the killing of a fellow man.

Those living in the southern part of Germany lost nearly all of their personal property, which was carried away by the marauders. The magistrates seemed to think that as these people were unwilling to go to war, they should at least pay the penalty by the loss of their goods. Many were pressed into the service, but they mildly and temperately, yet firmly, refused to serve. They said, in the language of the Bible, " We ought to serve God rather than men."

In the wars of Frederick the Great, the Inspirationists wrote much against the evils of wars. The position which they took may be summed up as follows:

I.   The teachings of Christ forbid war.

II.   The precepts and the practice of the apostles agree with the teachings of Christ.

III.   The early Christians were firm in their belief in the unjustness of war, and many suffered death in affirmation of this belief.

IV.   War is not a necessary evil, for if the people would not fight, ambitious rulers would either have to fight themselves, or dwell in peace and harmony.

V.   The general character of Christianity is wholly inconsistent with war, and its general duties are contrary to it.

A SKETCH OF A FEW OF THE MEMBERS NOT PREVIOUSLY
MENTIONED, WHO TOOK AN ACTIVE PART IN THE
SOCIETY IN THE EIGHTEENTH CENTURY.

One of the pillars of the church, not yet mentioned in this
paper, was Johann Philip Kämpf, a man who suffered great
hardships at the hands of relatives and friends, because he
cast in his lot with the Inspirationists.

Kämpf was born in 1688, in Sultzern, Gregorianthal, and
died at Homburg, 1753. His parents were pious people in
good circumstances. His father was mayor of Sultzern, also
senator from Münster. He was a man well-educated, a strict
Lutheran, honest and God-fearing, and was admired by all
with whom he came in contact. The son loved him almost
to veneration, and speaks of him with the most tender affection: — "My honest father, of whom I am not worthy to be
called his son!"

The father did not wish his son to apply himself to learning,
but preferred he should become a farmer, for he thought that
life to be the most independent and the most laudable.

At Münster, lived an old and learned minister by the name
of Faber, an intimate friend of Mayor Kämpf. These two
men had been elected by the school board to visit the city
schools, in order to conduct some preliminary examinations.
After an hour's tedious work, young Kämpf was called up
before the old preacher; the boy answered so fluently, without
displaying the least embarrassment, that the preacher was
struck with amazement. He told the father that such a boy
ought certainly to become a clergyman. The father replied
by asking how it was that "the clergy and the educated are
further away from God than the illiterate, and it takes more
persuasion to bring such persons back to God than others."
The preacher nodded his head and said this was an eternal
truth which he could not explain, but he still maintained that
the boy must acquire a thorough education. He went on to
prove this by quoting Scripture (Daniel XII, 3). This quota-
tion must have had the desired effect, for the boy was sent

to the University in Strasburg, where he soon distinguished himself for his quick perception and his easy mastery of the curriculum. Outside of his school hours, he pored over the classic authors, communed whole afternoons with the old philosophers, and spent whole nights reading and meditating upon the fathers of the church.

The boy had been brought up a Lutheran, but suddenly he changed his views. A preacher in Strasburg always ended his sermons by condemning the Pietists. This man became suddenly sick and finally died, praying God for mercy for having persecuted the Pietists. One of the students who saw this death-bed scene ran out into the University grounds, where the students were lounging, and told them what the preacher had said before he expired. This story went direct to Kämpf's heart.

As before he had pored over the classics, he now with equal enthusiasm pored over the works of Spener, Kempis, Arndt, and Böhme. He wanted to get at the root of these pietistic doctrines which the preacher had condemned. For a number of years these authors were the only companions of his solitude. This minute investigation satisfied him as to the truths of the doctrine, and the result was a book which he published, called " *Die Unchristlichen Gebräuche von Christ-kindlein unter den Leuten,*" a book setting forth true Christianity in a clear form, and showing the advantages to true religion which would ensue if Spener's doctrines were taken into the church. Comment and criticism were heaped upon Kämpf, for advocating such views, but the author, with true Saxon courage, would not retreat a step from the position he had chosen.

He maintained his ground so well in the controversy which ensued, that he was elected to the chair of philosophy in his alma mater. Kämpf accepted the appointment, and when he took the chair gave a disputation on true philosophy; this thesis made him more friends. Further investigation of this sublime subject opened his eyes to the falseness of learning when it is used to reason out things which God only

knows. He became disgusted with philosophy as it was
taught in the schools, where it took the place of religious
thought. There, belief in things divine was set aside, and
Rationalism had taken its place. It was at the heart of Rationalism that Kämpf directed his stored-up energies, yet without any marked success, for the plausible Rationalistic creed
had taken such a firm hold of the schools that all the energies
of one man could not move the barriers which were becoming stronger and stronger. Kämpf believed with Aristotle
that "whether you will not philosophize, or you can not
philosophize, you must philosophize." But Kämpf maintains
"that since there is a limit to all things, there is also a limit
reached in philosophy beyond which we have no right to
search, but must take for granted." He refused to speculate
on the region of God, the essence of the soul, and the origin
of the world. "When man begins to form hypotheses on such
sublime subjects, man tries to become equal to God." This
seemed to him to be a sin.

He finally gave up the chair of philosophy in Strasburg,
and accepted an invitation to become court preacher at Bühl,
in Elsass. The fame of the "preacher philosopher" soon extended over all Elsass, and people came from all parts of the
district to hear and to see the man who had stirred up the
German philosophers. His sermons were free from the
affectations of the age, they were delivered with all the bold-
ness which characterized the man, and king as well as peasant
received his full share of warning.

In 1716 J. A. Gruber and H. S. Gleim, who were engaged
in revival work, visited Bühl. One evening Kämpf was invited to dine with a friend, at whose house these men made their
home. After dinner was over and they were all seated in a large
drawing-room engaged in conversation, Gruber suddenly fell
into Inspiration. His words so affected Kämpf that he soon
after joined the Society. Kämpf had tasted all there was to
be had in life; he had acquired learning from all sources,
ranging from the expansive field of philosophy down to the
small store of folk-lore found among the peasants; but all this

learning did not satisfy, nor did it console him. True, he had preached for years and had aroused the people by his argumentative discourses, but still these scholarly sermons had not originated from conviction of heart, but were simply the product of his learning. They were sermons delivered without conviction, without the soul and the spiritual individuality of the man. The simple, plain, unostentatious sermon of Gruber possessed those elements so essential in religion; it came from pure conviction, and was devoid of affectation; it came from the soul, and lodged in the souls of his hearers.

From this time Kämpf became a changed man. He refused money for his preaching, though he continued to hold his place at court. A lady of high rank, related to the court, was visiting in Bühl and wanted to partake of the communion, but Kämpf refused to admit her to the communion table until she reformed her mode of life, which was of a questionable character. Such a refusal would have been applauded and admired if the person in question had been a peasant, but as she was one of the nobility, the act was looked upon as an insult. The minister was denounced as a religious fanatic, and finally dismissed from the service which he had gratuitously rendered.

Kämpf now took a course in medicine, and settled down in Bergzabern for the practice of his profession. He more and more felt the need of an open confession of faith, and in 1718 joined the Inspirationists. In the same year he received a call to become physician to the Swedish embassador Baron von Stralinheim, who lived at Zweibrucken, Bavaria; this offer he accepted. In a short time he became noted in the medical profession, was made director of the royal hospital and physician to Duke Gustaf, the friend of the fugitive Stanislaus, king of Poland.

Kämpf always associated with men of the court, men who perhaps despised his religion, but who admired his character, his great abilities, and his piety. Although he was absorbed in his profession, he still found time to make extended visits as a minister of the gospel. Because he worked as a minister instead of devoting his time to his chosen profession, he was exiled and came to Homburg, at which place he started a new meeting, which soon became prosperous. In 1739 the Crown Prince of Hessen was in Homburg, on his way to Russia. He heard of Kämpf, and soon persuaded him to become his physician. In Russia Kämpf also spread the doctrines of the Society, especially in St. Petersburg, where he remained for several years.

After his return from Russia he went again to Homburg, where he died in 1753. Kämpf wrote much on philosophy and religion, besides a long treatise on Inspiration.

William Ludwig Kämpf, son of the former, was also a physician of some note. In the affairs of the Society he took an active part. He died at Neuwied, 1779, at the age of 46.

Another of the pillars of the Society was Johann Casper Löw, born at Mühlhausen, Bavaria, 1692. He was descended from a godly stock of people, followers of John Huss, who had been compelled to flee from Austria on account of their religion. The family was in poor circumstances. The father was a linen weaver who toiled early and late in order to earn enough for the support of a large family. Johann was the youngest of thirteen children. When he was old enough to earn his own bread, he gathered together his little possessions and bade his parents farewell, as the other brothers had previously done. He received the blessings of the aged couple, who were greatly moved to see their last child leave,—their only solace in their declining years. But the son thought that he could no longer be a burden to them. With tears rolling down his cheeks he turned away from the scenes of his child-hood to battle with the world, with the actual realities of life. He travelled on foot, carrying under his arm a little bundle containing all his earthly possessions. He was about to return in despair, for he could find no work, when he found employ-ment as a cook with a royal family at Büdingen. He was an honest, faithful boy, and was soon esteemed by all who knew him. He remained in the service of this family many years, at last becoming chief cook. As his early education had been neglected, he now improved his opportunities so that he became well-versed in the literature and common branches necessary in his day for an ordinary scholar.

In 1714 he attended an Inspiration meeting, out of curiosity. He was greatly affected by it, for this seemed to be the religion of his parents and his grandparents, appearing in a new garb. This fact led him to investigate their doctrines, and he proved them to fully correspond to his own ideas of what religion ought to be. For several years he felt dejected, for he was certain that he lacked the power to withstand the ridicule of his associates if he should join the Society, and in not joining he felt he was sinning against God. In 1717 he attended an Inspiration meeting conducted by Ursula Mayerin, at Ronneburg. She seemed to realize what had been weighing on Löw's mind for years. She analyzed his feelings with great exactness, and then applied the remedy. Löw now became fully convinced, and joined the Society, having in the meantime lost his place in Büdingen on account of this conversion to the doctrines of the Society. In 1728 he became inspired for the first time, and from now to the time of his death, which occurred at Büdingen, 1775, he travelled much as a minister. He was the last one to depart of that little group which worked so gloriously in the beginning of the century. Löw has left but little in writing, but he left instead the character of a noble, upright man, who could say with Pericles, " I meet my doom with the consolation that I have injured no man." Löw's work was among the poor and depraved, where he labored assiduously during his long life of usefulness. He settled the petty disputes which often arose between members in the Society; he was always ready to lend a helping hand to the needy, and encouraged all in that godliness and morality which were reflected in his unsullied character.

A few others might be mentioned in connection with the founders. The descendants of these are still in the Society, where they work with the fervor and enthusiasm which were so characteristic of the older men. There occur the names of

M. Trautmann, a Swiss; Gottlieb C. Rall, who died in 1754; and Abraham Noé, from Anweiler, born 1764, died 1805. Gottfried Neuman was a theological student, having graduated from Leipsic and Halle. When he was about to enter upon his career as a minister in the Established Church, such feelings of responsibility came over him that he resigned his trust to another and withdrew from society and the church. After living in retirement for some time he joined the Inspirationists, where he worked continually, both as a writer and as a minister.

Johann Nicolaus Duill was also a minister in the Established Church from Eckershausen, Ysenburg, Hessen, who joined the little flock of pious believers in the beginning of the century. He did not travel as much as the others, due perhaps to a delicate constitution, but he worked faithfully among the members at home, while younger and stronger men went out into the world, "proclaiming the glad tidings of a new Jerusalem."

Blasius Daniel Mackinet, a relative of one previously mentioned, was an enthusiastic worker both at home and abroad. Of a lively disposition, and a jovial companion, he knew when to be serious and when not to be; bold in utterance, he was fearless and daring when he felt that it was right so to be.

George Melber was a well-to-do merchant in Heilbrom, Hessen, who, although not a preacher, was an organizer in temporal affairs. He was always willing to lend a helping hand to the needy, and gave advice and consolation to those in tribulation.

Anna Maria Schurr, a woman of much ability, was converted in 1726. She soon became a valuable minister, laboring with the other women formerly mentioned. She died in 1760, at the age of 75, her abilities and good health preserved to the last.

Jacob Hoffman, of Basel, became converted while Rock was making a religious visit in that part of Switzerland. Hoffmann died in 1763.

Simon Brangier was born at Niort, Poitou, in France, 1712,

of Protestant parents who had suffered much from religious persecution, but had not forsaken the place of their birth. Simon also loved the place where he was born, and where his relatives had been laid to rest. Finally the decree came that all the pious believers of Poitou who were not willing to change their creed, should be exiled from the district. A few submitted to the conditions of the decree rather than be driven away, but the majority, among whom was Brangier, gathered together their few earthly possessions and with sad hearts left everything that was dear to them behind, in order to find somewhere a new home where they could worship God according to the dictates of their own conscience.

Brangier, with a few others, finally settled down in Zweibrucken, Hessen. Here they found the Society of True Inspiration well represented. They inquired into the doctrines of the Society and found so much similarity with their own views that they joined and became influential members. Brangier travelled much in the capacity of minister and organizer. He followed Kämpf to St. Petersburg, where they organized a little meeting. But it seems that among the Russians they were not as successful as among their own people.

THE REVIVAL OF 1817.

After the death of Rock, in 1749, Inspiration ceased. The Society still had many eminent divines enlisted in its ranks, but they did not possess this remarkable gift.

Flourishing meetings were kept up in Ysenburg, Wittgenstein, Neuwied, Homburg, Switzerland, Elsass, and Würtemberg. The older men were passing away and the younger ones who took their places, although they may have had the ability, lacked the enthusiastic spirit of the older ones. They began more and more to lead a quiet life. They grew rich and fell back among the worldly. It had been prophesied that new men should arise to carry on the work taken up by Gruber and Rock, but years passed without any signs of the fulfillment of the prophecy.

The brilliant career of Frederick the Great, under whose reign these people had drunk the cup of bitterness to the dregs, came to an end. Frederick had labored unceasingly to bring about a union between the Lutheran and the Reformed churches, but his plans miscarried, owing to the influence of political events.

At the time of the Revolution in France the Society, though groaning under oppression, did not expect from its outcome a new regime, able to cure all diseases of the body politic. During this struggle, which did not cease until Wellington silenced the vanquished armies at Waterloo, the members were obliged to suffer all the calamities which only war can bring. The French and German armies marched and countermarched over the places of their habitation, making every spot a desert, taking even the men who were working in the fields and pressing them into service. It seemed that the Society would soon cease to exist, for the older men died and the younger ones lost courage.

The dawn finally came: the revival came, unnoticed and unheralded. It brought new blood and new life into the Society, and from this time its future was to a certain extent assured.

The principal persons in this revival movement were M. Kraussert, Barbara Heinemann, Christian Metz, Abraham Noé, Johannes Heinemann, Peter Mook, Martin Bender, Wilhelm Nordmann, J. G. Ziriazi, Frederick Müller, from Edenkoben, Philip and Wilhelm Mörschell, from Ronneburg, and Jacob Mörschell, of Neuwied, Philip Beck, from Pfalz, Peter Winzenried, Peter Hammerschneitt, Philip Sommer, and Gottlieb Ackermann.

The first who began to prophesy, after this gift had ceased for over half a century, was Michael Kraussert, of Strasburg. His gift was recognized and he began to travel and preach, again arousing the old enthusiasm, However, in a few years he fell back, and finally lost his power of prophecy.

The most remarkable person, perhaps, who was ever connected with the Society was Barbara Heinemann, a poor, ignorant peasant girl from Leuterville, Lower Elsass, where she was born in 1795. She was one of the first inspired in the revival, one who had experienced the oppression which the government practiced more and more towards the members of the Society during their last years in Germany, and she followed the little flock to America in search of freedom and a home. She experienced all the trials to which they were exposed in the first settlement, near Buffalo, New York, and she was one of the first to come to Iowa, where she again took up her work, a work which did not cease until 1883, when she was laid to rest, without any outward show but with much inward feeling, in the Amana cemetery, at the advanced age of eighty-eight.

Her parents were pious people. They were in such poor circumstances that Barbara never attended school a day in her life, but at the early age of eight was sent to a neighboring factory, where she earned a little pittance at spinning wool. In 1813, a financial crisis occurred, caused by Napoleon's endless wars. After the battle of Leipsic the entire country suffered from panic. The factory in which Barbara had worked for ten years was closed and she was compelled to go out as a servant.

While she worked in the factory she had been of a lively disposition; now a peculiar state of mind bordering on melancholy suddenly clouded her lively temperament. She gave up her work and returned home, in hope of improvement. She frequently attended church, for, if she engaged constantly in prayer, she thought this gloom might pass away. Once as she partook of the sacrament, the priest said, "Who is unworthy and drinks, he drinks judgment unto himself." This made a deep impression upon her mind, and she solemnly promised so to guide her life as to be acceptable to God.

She conversed with the priest and all the godly mothers of the neighborhood regarding the state of her mind, but no one could explain it satisfactorily, nor relieve her melancholy. One woman said she acted like the Pietists, of which people Barbara had never heard. She loved solitude and spent much of her time wandering about in the fields communing with God and nature. One night she had a dream telling her how her conversion was to take place. "I sat in a room at dusk," she says in her Memoirs, "contemplating the mercy of God; I saw my youthful companions without, joyful and happy, and anxious to have me join them; but I sat unmoved, not knowing whether to go or not, when I heard a loud voice which penetrated marrow and bone, bidding me remain. I began to feel easier, and perceived that God had heard my prayers." Feeling uncomfortable on account of this dream, she proceeded to Sulz, where a few Pietists were said to live.

She was kindly received by these people, who did all in their power to console and comfort her. She told her dream, which they believed would come true if she would only listen to God's voice when it was heard.

She remained with these people for several months, slowly improving in mind, when M. Kraussert came to the neighborhood on a religious visitation. Barbara was glad to find some one who took an interest in her depression of mind, some one who could explain to her all the trials she had passed through in the last few years. He thought that she would become inspired and speak in meetings. To become better acquainted with the Inspirationists and their doctrines, she accompanied M. Kraussert to Bergzabern, Bavaria. On Christmas day, 1818, at the age of 23, she became inspired for the first time, in one of their meetings. Although she knew nothing from books, she spoke in the language of the schools, for it was fluent, clear and free from error. Kraussert became subject to Inspiration and affirmed all she had said, feeling, as he did, that it came from God.

She joined the Society and went about doing religious work, when she was arrested, along with M. Kraussert and Christian Metz. All were accused of heresy by the city magistrate. They remained in prison only a short time, as nothing could be proved against them.

She became inspired in the meetings, in the fields, while at work, at home or on journeys. For this reason persons always accompanied her, to take down what she said while under this influence. These revelations are still read by the members of the Society for edification and consolation, and after a lapse of nearly a century they have lost none of their flavor.

This state of mind caused jerkings and twitchings of the body for a short time before she began to speak, so that she was conscious of what was coming on. She could prophesy with great exactness what was likely to take place. When she concentrated her mind upon those things which she wished to know, it caused a nervous exhaustion, from which she did not easily recover.

The persecutions Barbara Heinemann had to suffer at the hands of the magistrates were not all the trials she had to pass through. Members of the Society who were rich and influential were not pleased to have the poor, ignorant peasant girl looked upon as a prophetess and as a minister of the gospel. All sorts of accusations were brought against her. She patiently submitted to these wrongs, and she was for a short period expelled from the Society. The accusations, which were false, were withdrawn; the few who had conspired against her were expelled, and she was reinstated, to the comfort of the Society and her own consolation.

The Society was reorganized. Besides the twenty-one articles of E. L. Gruber, the twenty-four articles of Johann Adam Gruber were adopted as the basis of their faith. The members became more and more enthusiastic in the work, the Society increased in numbers, and everything pointed to a brilliant future.

In 1823 Barbara Heinemann was married to George Landmann. Her gift of Inspiration had ceased, and did not return until 1849; from that time she continued to be inspired until the time of her death.

This woman was the only one in the Society who possessed the gift of Inspiration, after the death of Christian Metz, in 1867, and since her death no one has so far been able to take her place. She was a woman who possessed many noble qualities; meek and patient in suffering, she knew how to comfort those in trouble; how to touch a tender spot in the hearts of those who were wayward and lukewarm in matters of religion; always keeping her presence of mind, she could censure without offence, and exhort without ranting; of an amiable disposition, she was respected and venerated by all who knew her.

All the education she received she acquired herself, without the aid of a teacher, and when she learned how to read and write her joy was great, for she felt an inward delight to be able to commune with God through the Holy Scriptures. Although she knew nothing of the philosophies of the schools, she could analyze the "common sense" philosophy of the heart. What she uttered during those periods when she was inspired, seems the product of deep thought, coming from the serene depths of a soul that understood the highest and noblest motives in man.

Christian Metz, a son of Jacob Metz, of Neuwied, previously mentioned, also became inspired about 1820. He was a man of much executive ability, and the temporal affairs of the Society were nearly all conducted by him, up to the time of his death in 1867.

The name Metz is of frequent occurrence in the history of the organization, from the time of its foundation. Originally from Elsass, whence Johann George Metz was driven on account of his religious views, in 1716,—it is in Hessen that the family for over a century toiled and suffered for the principles which the founder held dearer than home or native land.

Christian Metz was not only an organizer; he was a preacher and writer as well. He made five visits to Switzerland; visited Elsass, Lorraine, Saxony, and Würtemberg many times; in all these places he won converts to his cause. In 1824 Metz was prominent in winning over many Herrnhüters who had estranged themselves from that body.

In Würtemberg there lived a number of pious people called Michelians, named after the founder, Michel Hahn, a pious mystical preacher, who had exercised much influence by his reformatory measures. After his death the believers were scattered, not knowing what denomination to join, and too weak to continue the work their founder had begun. When Christian Metz happened to pass through that country on a religious visitation a few of them joined the Society. They did not long enjoy the peace and comfort they found within its protection, for the French government oppressed and persecuted all dissenters in Elsass and Strasburg, and they were driven out of France and came as fugitives to Germany, where they found a home with their fellow believers in Hessen.

In 1833 Switzerland took steps toward Conservatism, caused by a relapse of the revolutionary spirit of 1830. Oaths had to be taken in order to swear fealty to the government, and every able-bodied man at a certain age had to learn the art of war. Many families left their native land and came to Hessen. Two years later several more came; the most prominent of the new comers were Scheuner, Trautmann, Moser, Benedict and Hieronimus Gasser, and Aeshlimann.

From Basel came Burgy, Graf, Ladmann, Salathe, and Weckerling. Gottlieb Ackermann came from Lauenheim, in Saxony. His family belonged to the Gichtelians, followers of a revivalist by the name of Gichtel.

With all these exiles thrown upon the Society, without any means and for the most part without work, the members were in great perplexity. Christian Metz, far-sighted and thoughtful, came to the conclusion that the best method would be for the Society to lease some large estate, where the exiles could be put to work and make enough to supply their wants, the Society paying the rent.

The Marienborn castle, between Bergheim and Ronneburg, which formerly had belonged to the Herrnhüters, was leased by the Society. But this was not enough, for members kept coming from Würtemberg, from Elsass, and from Switzerland; besides it was not well to have the different nationalities together, as their dialects and customs were different. By 1834 three more castles with adjoining estates were leased, one at Armenburg, where the Swiss had found a home; another at Engelthal, where the Würtemberg exiles were placed; and still another at Haag.

For the use of these estates the Society paid an annual sum of 18,000 florins. As high as five and one-half florins were paid for the use of a morgen of land.

The members lived for the most part together in the castle or adjoining buildings, and in a large room in the castle meetings were held, and the children were taught; they worked the land together, sold the products and divided the proceeds equally. At first they did not eat at the same table, but when they saw that it would be cheaper to eat together this plan was adopted.

Here we have the first beginnings of the communistic life, which the Society afterwards adopted. It arose unconsciously, from small beginnings, with no thought of the results which would flow from it.

A few of the members were artisans, and preferred to work at their old trades rather than work on the estates. Therefore the societies rented a few factories, where those who were skilled in trades were placed. The members at the Castle of Haag leased a woolen mill, a grist mill, and an oil mill, the expenses being borne by the Society, which was taxed to its utmost in order to satisfy all bills and to keep the wolf from the door. In Armenburg a woolen mill was erected by the Society, so that the members could find employment.

For a time it seemed impossible for the Society to take care of all who came, but soon their woolen goods became famous throughout the country. They had adopted the motto, *"Honesty is the best policy,"* a motto which they have always lived up to in all their dealings. The goods were more and more in demand. It was found that they used the best material, and took the greatest care in the making of them.

In 1837 the first love feast since the revival of 1817, was held at Armenburg.

Jacob Dorr, of Bergheim, and William Metz, a cousin of

C. Metz, both joined the Society, in which they worked faithfully for the furtherance of their creed.

Many people belonging to other denominations came to visit the members of the Society, having heard or read much about their peculiar ways.

Once a number of pious people called Die Weisen ("*the Whites*"), because they dressed in white, perhaps to imitate the angels, came to Hessen. These people claimed to be inspired. They had a prophet who said he could foretell future events. But the members of the Society would not have anything to do with these people, who were undoubtedly religious fanatics, for they believed that the world would come to an end on a certain day, and the believers giving up work, patiently waited, clad in white, for the day when they should be taken to the other world. These were the forerunners of the Adventists. All their money was put into a common fund, on which they all lived. They assembled in the house of the prophet, where they spent entire days engaged in prayer. The prophet, with many others, was taken to prison where he died, when most of the others were released. These poor enthusiasts wandered about and finally came to Hessen where a few joined the Society.

Many of Die Weisen were good, christian people, who tried to live a godly life, but in their enthusiasm they undoubtedly carried their mode of worship too far.

There had been a contest fought in the courts years before, as to whether an affirmation could be made instead of an oath, and whether persons conscientiously could learn the art of war when their lives and their principles were those of peace. Some principalities had decided in favor of the Society, others against it. Hesse-Darmstadt had been the most liberal, and it was in this principality that the majority of them found a refuge. But enemies who were jealous of the success of the Society soon began to stir up a feeling of dissatisfaction among the ruling classes, and so the old liberties were little by little taken away.

When the year 1841 had arrived things had come to a crisis,

for encroachments had been made from all sides. The members assembled quietly and drew up a last imploring request to the Ministry at Darmstadt, begging for more freedom. They wished to affirm instead of taking an oath in civil matters, claiming that it was inconsistent with the Scriptures to take an oath. They wished to educate their own children, and were willing to support the State schools besides. Up to this time the children had been obliged to attend the óther schools, where instruction was nearly all of a character in accordance with the Established Church. They said they could not under any circumstances take up arms, believing it to be inconsistent with the Bible; therefore they could not conscientiously spend the best years of their lives in learning the art of war, which seemed so inconsistent with true religion.

It was decided that none of these requests could be granted. This decision seemed the death-knell to the very existence of the Society, for faithful believers had come as exiles and fugitives from many parts of Europe, and now their hope of toleration was destroyed.

But great changes had taken place in Europe from 1830 to 1840.

When the French for a third time discarded their king, altered their constitution and chose a "citizen king" for ruler, the elements of discontent were set in motion all over Europe. Kings trembled and ministers, narrow and superstitious, advised the rulers to press the yoke more firmly on the people, so that they would not rebel.

Revolts broke out in nearly every large city in Europe. The Poles rose in an unsuccessful attempt to throw off their shackles; the Belgians proclaimed their independence; while in Italy, Mazzini, the patriot, and prophet of Italian liberty, arose from obscurity; in England the Reform Bill, the slavery agitation, and Chartism were convulsing the public mind; but Germany, always conservative, rather fell back a step than took a stride forward in the march of freedom and reform.

Besides the unfortunate results which had directly or in--

directly come from this revolutionary spirit which had spread
discontent among some nations and freedom among others,
there were other causes which led to dissatisfaction and finally
removal upon the part of the Society of True Inspiration.

Land was too high for most of the members, who were in
moderate circumstances. To purchase wood was costly, and
there was no coal to be had. Rent for estates and factories
was exorbitant, and increased every year. During the summer of 1841 no rain fell, so absolutely nothing was raised.
The landlord wanted his rent as usual, regardless of the
failure of crops. Everything seemed dark and dreary, for
the leaders of the Society were unable to meet the demands
for money.

One day, as Christian Metz was walking over a hill, absorbed in meditation as to the future outlook of the Society,
he came within sight of the mills and estates that had been
rented. He heard the hum of the machinery, he saw the
toiling workmen bending under their heavy loads, he saw the
little children playing and shouting around the house doors;
he saw the women in the adjoining fields bending over the
sheaves, sickles in hand, trying to get something, even the
straw, in return for the summer's work. While he stood
there absorbed in thought, something "opened itself to him as
if a ray of light suddenly burst from heaven."[1] He felt that
one Hand was still powerful. 'If they only could have faith in
that divine Hand, all would be taken from the land of bondage
to a land of freedom, equality and fraternity.' Christian Metz
told some of his friends about this sudden glimpse into the
future. Others said they had had similar feelings, but dared
not express them.

On the 21st of July, 1842, one of the members became inspired, and it seemed to him that the members should all leave
their native land and should settle in one place, live under the
same laws, and adopt a "community of goods" which then had
many admirers in Europe. This movement had been caused
by the appearance of E. Cabet's book on Communism, called

---

1 *Inspirations Historie*, II., p. 112.

"*The Voyage and Adventures of Lord Causdal in Icaria,*" a book much like More's *Utopia.* Still more prominent was Fourierism which had become universal.

All the elders were summoned to meet at Armenburg, where they discussed the matter thoroughly but came to no decision. Another meeting was held at Engelthal, where this important matter was again discussed. It was plain enough to them that they would have to leave Germany on account of the severe measures of the government, and the failure of the crops of the preceding year, which had depleted their finances. They were still undecided where to go, but it seemed that the United States offered the best advantages.

Johann Adam Gruber had settled near Philadelphia over a century before, and had corresponded with members of the Society until the time of his death, 1763. It is not unlikely that they were acquainted with the Rappists, a small body of Protestants who had been driven from Würtemberg in 1803, and who under the guidance of their leader, George Rapp, had found a refuge and a home in America, where they had adopted a "community of goods," which they claimed was the doctrine of the primitive Christians. They settled at Economy, Pennsylvania, fifteen miles west of Pittsburg, where there is still a prosperous community. Another division of these people settled at Harmony, Posey county, Indiana; their property was sold to Robert Owen.

The Inspirationists probably knew of the Dunkers, who sprung up in Schwarzenau in 1708, about the time that they themselves began their existence. The Dunkers were persecuted and fled to Holland, where they remained until 1719, when twenty families landed in Philadelphia; soon more followed, and by 1842, they had congregations in nearly every state of the Union.

On the 14th of August, 1842, the elders decided that four men should be elected to look up a place for them in America or any other country suitable for a new home, where they could all live in common.

The four men selected for this difficult and responsible task were Christian Metz, G. A. Weber, Wilhelm Noé, and Gottlieb Ackermann, in whose hands was placed all power to act in matters concerning a suitable place, and concerning the amount of land to be purchased.

After a love-feast held at Armenburg, they bade each other farewell on the 5th of September, 1842. It was an affecting sight to see a thousand people or more assembled; in this large gathering every one shed tears, feeling that all would soon follow these leaders into a foreign land, where they knew hardships without number must be endured.

Wilhelm Mörschell and a son of Weber accompanied them to Bremen, where they had to wait six days for a vessel.

Ferdinand, the son of Weber, would not return, so they concluded to take him with them.

On the 20th of September they embarked on the sailing vessel *New York*, Captain Wächter; and Wilhelm Mörschell bade them God-speed and returned home.

The voyage lasted thirty-six days. The room they had was so small that part of them had to go to bed in order to give the others room to sit down. Finally another room was taken, but this was also uncomfortable. Ackermann became very sick, and this illness lasted a long time after he arrived at their place of destination.

They had two severe thunder-storms and many hard winds. The food-supply was nearly exhausted, and many of the passengers were sick when the ship finally reached New York, October 26th, 1842.

Here they were detained for some time on account of Ackermann's illness. While staying in New York, the Captain introduced them to a land-agent, Paulsen, who had land all over western New York and Pennsylvania. He offered them (as he said) a great bargain in Chautauqua county, New York, near Erie, Pennsylvania. He also gave them letters of recommendation to land-agents in Wisconsin.

They went by steamboat to Albany, and from Albany to Buffalo on a canal boat. The weather was cold, snow fell, and the rapidly forming ice impeded their progress. On

November 12th they reached Buffalo and found a German hotel, where they rested for several days.

The committee proceeded with Mr. Paulsen, the agent, to the land near Chautauqua Lake which he had offered them for sale. The journey was made by steamboat to Dunkirk, and thence across the country. They found the land comparatively worthless and distant from any available market, Erie being the nearest town of any size. The return-trip to Buffalo was made by road, and the project of settling at Chautauqua Lake was definitely abandoned.

This journey is spoken of in the records of the Society as one of great hardship, and indeed one can well imagine that the November storms and the ice-cold winds which prevail in the lake country during that most inhospitable of months must have rendered even that short voyage from Buffalo to Dunkirk one of some difficulty. Although the distance from Dunkirk to Chautauqua Lake is really an insignificant one when measured in miles, the wretched roads and the cold weather gave them an exaggerated idea of the inclemency of the climate and the bareness of the country. It is impossible not to reflect how different would have been the present surroundings of this now famous summer resort if the committee had decided upon this purchase. In place of that brilliant semi-religious, semi-fashionable place of resort, filled with throngs of sober and throngs of frivolous-minded people, the quiet of the monotonous life of the Community would have reigned around the shores of the lake, and dominated the adjacent country. But their refusal to purchase these lands was a wise one. The situation was at the time an isolated one, no railways, no canals, no good highways connected that remote (though not remote) district with the great thoroughfares east and west, and no prescience could have foreseen the future popularity of Chautauqua. In this, as in other things, the men who represented the Community showed themselves far-seeing, prudent, and equal-minded, with a view not only to the seclusion which might tend to preserve their religious doctrines in their purity, but to a sufficient opportunity for the development of their material strength and their increase in wealth.

After their return this experience with one land-agent had made them cautious, and at the same time had filled them with a certain discouragement, but Dorsheimer, their host in Buffalo, told them about the Indian Reservation near that city which was soon to be vacated by the Seneca tribe. This strip of land, amounting to several thousand acres, had been bought from the government by the Ogden Land Company, viz: Thomas Ogden, of New York City, Wadsworth & Sons, of Geneseo, and Joseph Fellows, of Geneva.

After a thorough investigation of the resources of the Seneca Reservation, a contract was made with Fellows, agent of the Land Co., for 10,000 acres at $10.50 per acre.

The contract was sent to Ogden to be signed, but he refused to recognize the sale Fellows had made. Metz, Ackermann, Weber and Noé, with Dorsheimer as interpreter, now had to go to Geneva to see Fellows; he could do nothing about the matter, but told them to see Wadsworth & Sons at Geneseo, who owned the controlling interest in the company. The Wadsworths were very courteous, but said that land had risen in value, and that it would be impossible to sell at the figures Fellows had given them; still if Ogden was willing to sell at that price, they would confirm the contract. They then returned to Buffalo to wait for a reply from Ogden.

By January, 1843, they had received no answer, and they wrote him that they would look for land farther west as they could wait no longer. Mr. Ogden immediately requested them to come to New York City, where all the stock-holders were to be present at a meeting, and might grant them favorable terms.

Once more they left Buffalo, but with small hope of any agreement. On the journey they discussed the feasibility of the undertaking. Noé thought 4,000 acres would be enough, while Metz maintained that the amount they had bargained for was not too much. They finally made concessions on both sides and put the amount down to 5,000 acres, which amount after much discussion and wrangling on part of the Land Company was bought for $10.50 per acre, setting the limit this time within six miles of Buffalo. It would have been better if they had bought the 10,000 acres, for nearly all this same land was afterwards purchased at a much higher price.

They wrote to Germany rejoicing over their good fortune, but they were ignorant of the trials which were to be endured before the land could be called their own.

The Indians as soon as they heard of the sale began to show signs of hostility. Perhaps it is due to this fact that there had been so few buyers, for the people around Buffalo knew Indian character too well.

After this purchase Metz and Ackermann made a visit to Galion, Crawford county, Ohio, where there existed a small society of Germans, many of whom they had known in the Fatherland.

It has been stated in other articles upon the history of the Community that the communistic mode of life was in vogue at Galion, and that Metz and Ackermann made a study of its practical workings with a view of employing it or not in their own enterprises as the results at Galion seemed favorable or unfavorable. This view of the case is not taken by the members of the Community. They deny the existence of communism at Galion, and therefore any influence from it upon their own future. This visit was simply a friendly one made to see old friends, to observe the country, and to fill up the time of enforced inactivity. It may be said, however that Metz and Ackermann found the country rich and the German settlement prosperous, and after a visit of six weeks returned to Buffalo.

On their return they found that fifty of their number had already arrived from Germany. No preparation had been made to receive them, for they were not expected until later. The men were set to work erecting houses, while the older people and the women were permitted to stay in the old log huts which the Indians had abandoned.

On May 1st, 1843, the first village of a communistic nature

was laid out, much after the manner of the old German village. It was called Ebenezer (*Eben*, a stone, and *ezer*, meaning help), no doubt from the fact that there was much similarity in their own history to the circumstance mentioned in I Samuel, vii, 12, where it is stated that Samuel set up a monumental stone as a memorial of divine assistance in a battle against the Philistines; their battle had been a combat for truth and for freedom of conscience, which had been denied them in their native land, and which they now hoped to enjoy unmolested in the land of freedom.

In the same year two other villages were laid out which were called Upper and Lower Ebenezer, the first being named Middle Ebenezer.

The members continued to come in parties of fifty during the remainder of the year. Some came by way of Bremen, others via Antwerp, and still others via Havre. The latter route was the best, as provisions were furnished by the company, and the vessels were better in many ways. Those who came by Bremen and Antwerp had to furnish their own provisions, the ships were slow sailers, and consequently the emigrants often suffered from hunger.

During the summer of 1843 a large meeting-house was erected. Several school houses and many dwellings were built from the rough logs which were cut in the timber. A saw mill was also erected and operated for their own use.

The Indians were enraged as they saw these people planting and building and threatening to make short work of them, and the settlers applied to Fellows, the land agent, who had promised that the Indians should soon depart for the West. Fellows arrested a few Indians because they hauled and sold wood which belonged to the Ebenezer Community. The Indians in return claimed that the Community had no deed to the land, and therefore had no right to cut trees on it.

Matters went from bad to worse, and finally a council of arbitration was decided upon. Metz, Noé, and Weber appeared for the Community, and John Seneca with his chiefs and Osborne, their lawyer, represented the Indians.

The Indians wanted to be paid for their land a second time, to which the Community would not consent, for the Land Company had bought both the government right and the Indian-claim. The Indians, incited by bad white men and poor whiskey, would not make concessions, and thus ended the first congress of peace without accomplishing any result.

The factories in Germany had been built by the Society, but were managed by the poor exiles from France and Switzerland who were allowed all the profits. Here we may perhaps see the first unconscious step towards Communism. It was clearly seen that all these people could never acquire homes of their own, even if the Society paid the passage across the ocean. The welfare of the Society depended upon unity, and this could be best accomplished if the communistic plan were adopted. It was therefore decided that all the money should be turned into a common fund, and that each contribution should be returned without interest whenever the contributor wished to leave the Society. A few of the members were wealthy, but they gave up every penny in their possession without grumbling, feeling that it would be an act of charity, a blessing and a lasting benefit to hundreds of poor people who did not possess anything they could call their own.

By the end of 1843 three hundred and fifty persons had arrived. Those remaining in Germany were trying to dispose of their property, but they were not successful. The landlords at Laubach and Büdingen were unwilling to take back their estates when they heard that the members were about to leave. The members in America needed money to pay for the land, but none could be raised, since they were unable to sell their German property at any price.

In this crisis C. L. Meyer, from Zoar, Ohio, joined the Community. He became of great value to them, as he knew English perfectly, and also had a knowledge of law, which was of the utmost importance in the endless contest with the Land Company on one hand and the stubborn Indians on the other.

By April, 1844, the purchase price for the Reservation had

to be at Washington. The Ogden Land Company could not meet the demand and thus fell back on the Community, which by credit and loans raised a sum of $50,000, which was sent to Washington. Still the Community had no deed to the land. Becoming anxious about the title, Metz and Meyer went to New York City to investigate the matter. The Land Company could give no deed, since the title had not yet passed into their hands.

On their return to Buffalo they became still more discouraged at receiving a legal document from the attorneys of John Seneca, warning them to vacate the lands within one week, or there would be trouble. To pay $50,000, nearly the entire sum, and then to be driven away seemed almost unendurable, but they did not know what to expect from the treacherous Indians.

Another council of arbitration was held, which resulted as unfortunately as the first, for the Indians were supported by able lawyers, and had imbibed firewater so freely as to make the scene doubly interesting and exciting.

The Community now appealed to the government at Washington. The Indians were ordered to leave for the homes assigned them in the West, but they were in no hurry, and brought their case before the courts of New York, and after a period of several years the case was decided in favor of the Ebenezer Community by Judge Hall.

This decision put an end to the Indian troubles, which had been very annoying; although they never led to bloodshed, feelings of intense hatred on part of the Indians, who were stirred up by many of the whites, placed the Community in jeopardy if at any time an outbreak had occurred.

In June, 1844, two hundred and seventeen members came on the ship Florida via Havre; and in the following year Wilhelm Mörschell, Ernest Klein, G. Döller, C. Wilhelm, and many others, came by the same route.

This put an end to the emigration, and from this time on only a few came now and then.

More than eight hundred persons had come over, and all

had found comfortable homes and were well pleased both with the country and the communistic mode of life which the Society had adopted.

Many remained in Germany, some, because they were in good circumstances and were surrounded by relatives and friends with whom they could not part; in others, love of home and native land were too strong,—they felt bound to the soil from which they sprang, and could not be torn away from it. The communication between the two countries ceased by degrees, and has now become nearly extinct. This is due to the fact that the members in Germany fell away, and the younger ones did not follow in the steps of their fathers.

The constitution was ratified by the members on the 15th of February, 1845, and the Community was incorporated by the laws of the State. In August of the same year a warranty deed for the land was obtained.

Improvements were made, two saw mills, two woolen mills, and several factories were erected, while the amount of land was increased to between 8,000 and 9,000 acres. This was all the land they could obtain at moderate prices.

Among them were found skillful workmen representing all trades. There were carpenters, blacksmiths, tailors and jewelers. Implements and machinery were brought from Germany. It must be borne in mind that these persons came in sailing-vessels, when a passenger was allowed any amount of luggage, and canal-boat charges were about the same whether a passenger owned 100 or 1000 pounds. They took advantage of the opportunity.

The majority of the members who had come to America belonged to the sturdy peasant class of Germany, that class which forms the "bone and marrow" of all governments. They came to this land of freedom to adopt an entirely new mode of life; they had no experience in this new scheme which they wanted to adopt; they had but scanty means; they knew nothing of the language, the laws or business methods of the country; still they possessed one advantage over the other societies which had adopted similar methods;

the leaders of this society were neither agitators nor theorists,
—like Cabet and Owen—but they were sagacious, far-sighted
men, with much practical knowledge, something worth more
than all the high-flown speculative theories in existence. It
is due to the executive abilities of the trustees that the Society
has been so successful financially.

Notwithstanding their prosperity at Ebenezer, the elders
preferred another locality where cheaper land could be obtained,
and in 1855 the Society elected C. M. Winzenried, John
Beyer, Jacob Wittmer, and Friedrich Heinemann, to go West
in search of a favorable place for a new colony.

REMOVAL TO IOWA.

The Community had expressed no views as to where this
committee should go, but it was understood that the land must
lie at least west of Chicago. They thought of going to Wisconsin, but as a new railroad had just been completed to Davenport,
and the tide of emigration flowed in that direction, they followed the mighty army of land-seekers.

From Davenport they went to Muscatine, and from that
place up the Iowa River on a steamboat to Iowa City, a boom-
ing town, the capital of the state, where land agents flourished
and where boomers grew rich in the practice of their trade.

There was then no railroad nearer than Davenport, but the
stage coach and the Iowa River, which was then a good-sized
stream where steamboats plied back and forth, brought the
town into contact with the rest of the world.

The country was beautiful, the rolling prairies to the west
were for the most part still untouched by the advance guard
of civilization. The farther west the members came, the
more beautiful appeared the country. There were only a few
settlers in Iowa County, and these were along the timber.

It was only in 1843 that the Indians relinquished their claims
to the land; and in the following year, according to *Andreas'
Atlas*, the first settlement was made near the present site of
Homestead, by Lineas Miles and John Burgett.

At Homestead, then a post office connected by a stage line

with Davenport and Des Moines, the members remained for some time making excursions to different parts of the county.

Any amount of land could be purchased for from $1.25 to $5.00 per acre, both from the government and from the scattering settlers who were willing to sell at a small profit.

The members sent letters home describing the country in glowing terms. They saw many advantages which Ebenezer did not possess. Land was cheap and many thousand acres could be purchased in one strip, which was impossible in New York. For farming Iowa was superior to New York; and the rise in the value of land would probably be much greater.

There was another reason why Iowa seemed so much superior to Ebenezer. These sagacious men saw clearly that to preserve the purity and obedience of their members it was necessary to live, as much as possible, secluded from the world. To be near a growing city like Buffalo, where the members, especially the younger ones, were exposed to all the temptations of city life, was not the place for a religious and communistic society. For this reason, more than for any other, they preferred some secluded, quiet place in the West, where they could practice the doctrines of their creed undisturbed, and carry on communism without coming in contact with the rest of mankind.

The natural advantages of the place they had chosen offered facilities superior to any other place they had visited. The alluvial soil (bottom land) along the Iowa River is the richest in the state; the river furnished plenty of water for their stock and was large enough to drive any kind of machinery they wished to erect. The splendid timber,— oak, hickory, walnut, and maple,— would not only supply them with fuel, but with building material, which was then difficult to obtain, for the railroad extended only to Davenport. The clay was excellent for the manufacture of brick; limestone was found along a few bluffs,— enough to supply them with lime until better railroad facilities could be obtained. These were soon to come, for the capital had been located at Fort Des Moines during this year, and there the legislature met for the first time, in 1858.

The news from Ebenezer was favorable, and the Society, without further deliberation, bought a large strip of land, amounting to nearly 18,000 acres, which was afterwards laid out in a township by itself. The government land was worth from $1.25 to $2.50, and that owned by settlers from $3.00 to $5.00 per acre.

As soon as this immense tract of land had been purchased, the bravest of the Ebenezer Community set out for the country they expected to make their permanent home.

A large number went by steamboat to Chicago, and from there by rail to Davenport, from which place they had to go by stage direct to Homestead. Others who brought horses, cattle and implements drove across the country, arriving much later than the first party.

In the same summer (1855) a town was laid out on a beautiful sloping hillside, about one mile north of the Iowa River, near a charming little lake of about 200 acres, and with a stream (Price Creek) running through the village.

No more beautiful spot could have been chosen, and the natural advantages were also favorable—running water, plenty of timber, and a healthy location. On this spot all the hopes of the future were centered; here all was risked for the sake of obtaining a home. They had but little on which to rely, but they trusted to "strong hands and willing hearts" and began to clear the soil, to dig out the stone from the quarries and to put it into substantial buildings, which are still standing, as strong as ever, having defied wind and weather for nearly half a century.

A suitable name for the village was wanted, and as ten years previously they had gone to the Bible for a name, so once more they consulted the sacred Book, which is the cornerstone of their faith, for another name which would be appropriate. The hill called Amana described by Solomon in his Song (chap. iv, 8), resembles, perhaps, in beauty of surroundings, the place to which the members gave the same name,—but there is a meaning in the word Amana, which undoubtedly led them to select it. It means, "remain true,"—a motto from which they have never wavered. Mr. Nordhoff, in

his *"Communistic Societies of the United States,"* says that one
of the members took the Bible and it fell open where Solomon
speaks of this hill; therefore, he says, the village was named
Amana. This statement the elders of the Society strenuously
deny.

It was inconvenient to work all the land and live in one
village, nor was it desirable to have many people congregated
in one place. Therefore other towns were laid out as fast as
the people came from Ebenezer.

West Amana, five miles west of Old Amana, and South
Amana, six miles southwest of Amana, were begun in 1856;
High Amana in 1857, East Amana in 1860, Homestead in
1861, Middle Amana in 1862, and a new South Amana, half a
mile south of the old town, on the Chicago, Milwaukee & St.
Paul Railroad, in 1883. Homestead was an old post office
and village. This, the Society bought when the Rock Island
Railroad was extended through in October, 1861.

It was nearly ten years before the last members of the
Society came from Ebenezer to Iowa, having then sold all
their property in that place. Twelve hundred in all had
crossed the states which lie between New York and the Iowa
River.

In 1857, the third Constitutional Convention met at Iowa City,
to frame a new Constitution for the State. The members of
the Society had not yet drawn up any articles of incorporation,
for they wished to see the outcome of the Convention; neither
did the members buy more land, for they had an idea that the
framers of the Constitution would perhaps not recognize large
corporations.

On the 5th of March, 1857, that body completed its work,
which was approved by the people in the next year.

Article VIII, Sec. 1, of that Constitution says: No corporation shall be created by special laws; but the General Assembly
shall provide, by general laws, for the organization of all corporations hereafter to be created."

Article VIII, Sec. 12, says: "The General Assembly shall
have power to amend or repeal all laws for the organization
or creation of corporations, or granting of special exclusive

privileges or immunities, by a vote of two-thirds of each branch of the General Assembly; and no exclusive privileges, except as in this article provided, shall ever be granted."

In 1859 the Society drew up its articles of incorporation, and assumed the name of the "Amana Society." In New York they had assumed the name of "Ebenezer Community." The name, as a religious body, " Society of True Inspiration," by which they had been known in Germany, was still retained.

They were incorporated under an act of the General Assembly, entitled "An act for the incorporation of benevolent, charitable, religious and scientific societies,' approved March 22, 1858.

"ARTICLES OF INCORPORATION" OF THE "AMANA SOCIETY."

STATE OF IOWA, IOWA COUNTY,— SS:

To all Whom these Presents shall Come, Greeting:

KNOW YE, That William Mörschell, Charles M. Winzenried, Christman Wilhelm, Christian Metz, Theobald Heimburger, John Beyer, Jacob Whittmer, Jacob Schnetzler, Samuel Scheuner, George Walz, Jacob Winzenried, Joseph Elzer, and Peter Haldy, all of lawful age and citizens of the United States, and a majority of us citizens of the State of Iowa, and County of Iowa, for the purpose of forming ourselves into a religious and charitable society, for the benefit of ourselves, our associates and successors, under and by virtue of an act of the General Assembly of the State of Iowa, entitled "An act for the incorporation of benevolent, charitable, religious and scientific societies," approved March 22,

---

1 See McClain's Annotated Code of Iowa, Ed. of 1888, Secs. 1653–1664. Sec. 1649 has the following about the duration. 'Corporations organized under this chapter shall endure for the period of fifty years from and after their organization unless sooner dissolved by a vote of three-fourths of all the members thereof or by operation of law.' This amendment is not found in the Revision of 1860, but has been passed since, and consequently does not apply to the Amana Socieiy which may endure any length of time; but the General Assembly may, at any session, fix a time when all such corporations shall be dissolved.

1858, do hereby certify that this society shall be known in law by the name of *Amana Society*. That the principal place of business of the Society shall be in Iowa county, in the State of Iowa. That the principal object of this Society shall be to promote the temporal and spiritual welfare and happiness of its members. That the principal business of this Society shall be to purchase and receive real and personal property, to use, own, and carry on agricultural and mechanical pursuits, to build and erect on said real estate villages, churches, school houses, factories, and make such other buildings and improvements, and carry on and perform such other business as may be deemed essential to the well-being, happiness, and prosperity of this Society.

That the legislative or managing department of this Society shall consist of thirteen trustees, who shall be elected annually at such time and in such a manner as may be specified in its by-laws. That the executive department of this Society shall consist of one director, one vice-director, and one secretary, the vice-director only acting in the absence of the director and performing his duties,— who shall be elected by the trustees and out of their number, and hold office for one year, and be elected at such times and perform such acts and duties as may be required of them by virtue of the by-laws of said Society. And that the following persons are to act as officers of said society for the first year of its existence, viz.: William Mörschell, Sr., Charles Winzenried, Christman Wilhelm, Christian Metz, Theobald Heimburger, John Beyer, Jacob Whittmer, Jacob Schnetzler, Samuel Scheuner, George Walz, Jacob Winzenried, Joseph Elzer, Peter Haldy.

In witness whereof we have hereunto set our hands and seals this 8th day of December, A. D. 1859.

WILLIAM MÖRSCHELL, CHARLES WINZENRIED,
CHRISTMAN WILHELM, CHRISTIAN METZ,
THEOBALD HEIMBURGER, JOHN BEYER,
JACOB WHITTMER, JACOB SCHNETZLER,
SAMUEL SCHEUNER, JOSEPH ELZER,
GEORGE WALZ, JACOB WINZENRIED,
PETER HALDY.

State of Iowa, Iowa County,— ss:

I do hereby certify that before me, William H. Wallace, county judge in and for said county, personally appeared the above named William Mörschell, Sr., Charles M. Winzenried, Christman Wilhelm, Christian Metz, Theobald Heimburger, John Beyer, Jacob Whittmer, Jacob Schnetzler, Samuel Scheuner, George Walz, Jacob Winzenried, Joseph Elzer, Peter Haldy, who are personally known to me to be the identical persons who signed the above and foregoing instrument as affidavits, and acknowledged the same to be their voluntary act and deed for the uses and purposes therein signed.

Witness my hand and seal of said county, at Marengo, the 8th day of December, A. D. 1859.

W. H. WALLACE, *County Judge.*

Recorded December 13, 1859.

E. H. HENDERSHOTT,

County Recorder.

By A. B. ESHLEMAN, *Deputy.*

When the articles of incorporation were adopted, a well written constitution similar to the Ebenezer constitution was prepared and approved.[1]

Every effort was directed to paying off the debt they had contracted. Improvements were made on the lands; the wet lands were drained and the timber lands were cleared. Factories of different kinds were erected, but Price Creek did not furnish the necessary water for the mills at Old Amana and in 1863 a canal was dug from the Iowa River so as to supply Amana with water power. The canal was nine miles long, and it took more than three years to complete the great undertaking. An artesian well was begun, which is 1600 feet deep and yields a fine flow of warm, sulphuric water. It is used in the dye works. Another well was started on a high hill near South Amana, but although they worked for several years, they have so far been unsuccessful in obtaining a flow.

---

1 See *Appendix A.*

Two large grist mills were erected, one at Old Amana, the other at West Amana. These were of the greatest importance to the farmers in the vicinity, for there were no other mills nearer than Cedar Rapids and Iowa City, and for a distance of fifty miles to the west there were none at all. Every village had its saw mill, machine shops, and store, all of which were of great importance to the surrounding country.

Among the many noble pioneers of Iowa, who suffered and toiled for the younger generation, we may class the members of the Amana Society. They suffered the hardships of frontier life, they worked and toiled, and helped to build up the state and make it what it is to-day,— one of the foremost in the West. They were the first to erect factories, and while many others did so later and failed, the hum of the machinery in Amana is still heard and the Amana goods are sold throughout the United States.

The Calico Print Mills were erected in Old Amana. They color and print from 3,000 to 4,000 yards daily. The heavy cotton goods are manufactured in the South for the Society. These are called "blue print" and have a great reputation throughout the country.

Two woolen mills were also erected, one in Old Amana, and another in Middle Amana, where nearly 3,000 yards of woolen goods are made daily. They have over 3,000 sheep, but these do not supply them with enough wool, as they use over half a million pounds annually. They receive wool from Texas, Colorado, and sometimes from Australia. Their woolen goods are made with the greatest care and of the best material. There is no "piece work" method here, for everything is done well, without the rush and hurry which we see in other factories. Their goods are the best in the market, and the following expression is often heard: "Colony goods, full width, a yard wide." Six agents are on the road selling their goods, which are in demand from Maine to the Pacific.

Great quantities of flour are sold annually. They have soap factories, starch factories, hominy mills, and book-binderies.

Conrad Schadt, a well-known chemist, makes great quantities of pepsin, which by actual test is considered the best in the market. Mr. Schadt was the first man west of Chicago who began the manufacture of this article.

The Society has three physicians who look after the sick and feeble, viz.—Dr. Winzenried, who lives at Old Amana, a graduate of Rush Medical College, class '65; Dr. Hermann, of Middle Amana, a graduate of the medical department of the State University of Iowa, class '81; and Dr. Mörschell, of Homestead, State University of Iowa, '88.

The presidents of the Society since the removal to Iowa have been C. M. Winzenried (1855–81), J. Beyer (1881–83), Friedrich Mörschell (1883–89), Jacob Whittmer (1889–91), and P. Trautmann (1891–), the present incumbent.

The trustees, thirteen in number, are elected annually by the eligible citizens, twenty-one years of age. The trustees elect a president, vice-president, and secretary, from their number. There are eighty elders, who look after the spiritual welfare of the Community. They take turns in conducting meetings on Sundays and Wednesdays, and the prayer meetings held every evening.

During the war the Society petitioned Congress to be exempted from military duties. In 1863 Congress passed an act that by paying $300 a man could be exempted from military duties. This the members accepted in lieu of a special act and much money was paid out of their general fund to defray these expenses.[1]

In 1867, Christian Metz, the pioneer and main-stay of the Society since 1817 was laid to rest, and in 1883 Barbara Heinemann Landmann died, in her eighty-eighth year. These two were the only members who have been inspired during the existence of the Society in America. No one since then has been inspired, but the writings which they left behind are read in their meetings, for edification and solace.

---

1 This purchase of substitutes for those who were drafted has afforded the Society regret, and it has seemed to the members that it was perhaps inconsistent.

THEIR RELIGIOUS DOCTRINES.[1]

They believe in the inspiration of the Bible and take it as the corner-stone of their faith, trying to live according to the teachings of Christ and the Apostles.

They think that as God revealed hidden things through visions, dreams and by revelations in olden times, He can do so now.

They believe in Inspiration, and maintain that Inspiration can take place now as well as formerly. Inspiration, according to their ideas, "is a supernatural influence of the spirit of God on the human mind, by which persons are qualified to set forth divine truth," The one who becomes subject to Inspiration must have a "pure heart, a free soul without prior judgment, meek and obedient to divine will."

They believe that there is false as well as true Inspiration, and that prophesying did not cease with the Apostles.

They think the ministry of the gospel depends on Inspiration, and is not limited by class or sex. Therefore all members have an equal right to teach and exhort in public meetings; they think that if one is not led by the right spirit, no system of theological training can fit one to explain Scriptures. With them, "the Holy Ghost is sought from within, not from without."

They believe in prayer, both in meetings and at home in the closet. It is the "spontaneous expression of the soul which should not be fettered by any fixed or prescribed formula."

They do not believe in the Trinity as three distinct persons, but they reverently believe in the Three conceived of as One.

They do not believe in a purgatory, nor in a millenium in this life; nor in predestination.

They believe in the resurrection, in a reward for the good and punishment for the wicked.

They do not baptize with water, for they believe that baptism is purely spiritual.

---

[1] From their Catechism and other books.

They believe in and use the Lord's Supper, but only as a symbol of an inward feasting with the Lord. It is not used at any stated time or place, but after severe trials, or misfortunes; for the strengthening of the young members; in the commemorating of the suffering of Christ. Several days spent in prayer are necessary in order to participate in this rite.

They practice feet-washing, and have love feasts, much in the manner of the primitive Christians.

They believe war to be inconsistent with christianity,—i. e., with the teachings of Christ and the Apostles.

Oaths are inadmissible, since they were forbidden by Christ.

They use salutations, but object to frivolous plays as recreations which divert the mind from God.

Singing is indulged in at meetings and at home, for edification, but instrumental music is forbidden.

In dress they are plain and simple.

The burial customs are simple, without the ostentation of many other denominations. No costly monuments are used, but only a small slab of wood, painted white, bearing an inscription of the name and age of the deceased.

They do not believe in prayer for the dead nor in any outward form of mourning, but the memory of the departed members is cherished with more than filial affection in the hearts of friends,—something worth more than hired mourners and outward show.

COMMUNISM.

This subject has been so fully treated by so many able writers, that it would be folly to discuss it at length. However a few words may be said neither against nor for the system, but to show how it has been carried out by this Community.

Wolsey gives three reasons why a community of goods is adopted:

1st. That similarly disposed persons may come together and lead a life, which they could not lead among their fellowmen.

2d. Because some persons have revolutionary ideas they wish to promulgate.

3d. Because others have Utopian plans for the rectification of society.

The first of these three is the *raison d'être* of the Amana Society.

The communities founded in the United States have nearly all had glorious beginnings, but the results have rarely been satisfactory. Of them all, the Shakers, who left England in 1774, are the oldest and the largest, but they have dwindled to less than one-half; numbering now about 2,500. From 1774 to 1843 eleven societies had been founded, nearly all of which have been total failures. The average duration of eight was one and a half years. Since 1843 thirty-five communities have been organized on Fourier's plan, and the greater number of these have also been compelled to disband for various causes.[1]

Of two communistic societies in Iowa, both came to this State about the same time; both had similar advantages, but how different the results. The French Icarian community founded by Cabet in Texas on industrial methods was moved to Illinois, and from thence to Adams County, Iowa. Cabet, like Owen, substituted, for religion, reason as the corner-stone. Enjoyments, such as the theatre, music and dancing, were encouraged.

These mere social ties do not seem sufficiently strong to bind men closely and firmly together, as was proved in the Brook Farm experiment; quarrels arise and finally dissolution becomes the last resort. Albert Shaw in his *"Icarian Community"* says: "Party strife broke up the Icarian School in France, it divided the colony in Texas, rent the Society to pieces in Nauvoo, and scattered it Iowa." There still exists an Icarian Community in Adams County, Iowa, with about sixty-five members, and another branch called the Icarian-Speranza Community is established near Coverdale, California.

---

[1] For statistics of the above see Hinds.

The Amana Society has not increased rapidly, but since the adoption of a community of goods there has always been progress in the right direction. More than eight hundred came across the sea and formed the Ebenezer Community, and nearly twelve hundred made their way to Iowa, while at present it numbers about seventeen hundred, with 25,000 acres of land, thousands of cattle, and several mills and factories.

The number in Iowa from 1861 to 1891, taken by decades, is as follows:

> January 1st, 1861 — 572 members.
> "   "   1871 — 1466   "
> "   "   1881 — 1521   "
> "   "   1890 — 1660   "
> "   "   1891 — 1688   "

The members have never held "that the ownership of property is a crime," neither have they belonged to that dreamy class of idealists who continually appeal to sentiment in order to achieve success. Their Teutonic instinct of individuality made them preserve much of their independence, and this they still retain; they never belonged to that class which has nothing at stake, and therefore stirs up insurrections because they have nothing to lose and may have much to win. The Communism of this Society has been founded upon that sober, old christian idea of love which Christ and the Apostles gave to the world.

Some of their ideas upon this subject may be formulated as follows:

a. Religion is the only bond which can unite men in true fellowship.

b. If this is the fundamental doctrine of a Communistic society it will succeed.

c. When Communism is attempted by those who reject a God, or, admitting His existence, deny His interest in human affairs, then it must fail.

d. Reason alone, without a religious and moral obligation,

can not bind men into a community which shall be lasting, harmonious or advantageous.

This bond of religion may probably be considered as the most potent and efficient element of several which have contributed to their success.

Second in importance perhaps is their conception of Communism and their mode of government. The success of a Communistic society does not depend so much on the learning as on the practical common sense of its officers and its members. The truth of this postulate is evident from the history of the societies formed by Cabet and Owen. These were made up, to a great extent, of men of learning, or at least of education, who sacrificed their earthly possessions in the hope of realizing a Utopian dream. The Brook Farm is another instance of the failure of persons of culture and refinement to reform society. The history of the Brook Farm is too well known to bear repetition, but the names of its members will always be a testimony to the fact that theory and successful practice are very far from being the same thing, and that the wisest of philosophers may make the worst of practitioners. New Harmony and Brook Farm were failures—in spite of the wealth, the learning and the high social position of their members; the German Inspiration Community, which has never boasted of the learning of its members, and which can not point to great authors nor to splendid lineages as among its historic treasures, has succeeded, partly, because it possessed, not the elements of outward display, but others more essential to success—industry, frugality and perseverance.

Nearly all other communities have been founded on broad democratic principles with "fraternity and equality" as the war-cry. They have embodied a principle which found its highest attempted expansion at the time of the French Revolution, and signally failed. It is a principle, or a theory rather, for it can hardly be called a principle—it is a theory, which to be realized must presuppose a state of affairs approaching what may be called millenial. "Equality and fraternity" can of course be carried to a certain extent, but they must recognize in their turn, as everything else must, the limitations of human nature. They must recognize the existence in humanity of one potent element which will always prevent their perfect development, and this is the element of self. Self-abnegation may and can be carried to great lengths—in a monastery; in practical affairs it sinks to the measure of the average character of the average member of society. Enthusiasts and dreamers, dwellers in the clouds, recluses, no doubt may see visions and dream dreams of an absolutely altruistic world—or if not of such a world, at least of a corner where the throbbings and tumult of selfishness yield to the magic of equality and of brotherhood, but the Brook Farm experiment proves, to instance this only, that, even if such an idea be attempted to be realized, enthusiasm will quickly cool and that the members will be given up to faction and party strife.

The Amana Society, on the contrary, has never embodied these Utopian ideas; it is founded, as has been said, upon a basis more sober and less fanciful; it does not endeavor to make human beings more perfect than humanity is capable of being; it rests upon the principles of brotherhood which are taught in the Bible, and not upon those which philosophy has imagined may exist. If Communism can ever be successful it must proceed upon its way in accordance with the limitations of human nature; it can not reckon upon attributes of character which might belong to angels, but are not found among men; it must develop in accordance with, and not in defiance of existing conditions. The failure of most Communistic societies may be traced to the unpractical, theoretical and inchoate ideas of their founders, to the false views of human nature which have usurped the place of true ones, and to the belief that the prejudices of humanity may be, in an instant, reformed or annulled by circumstances. The falsity of this doctrine has been proved over and over again, and human nature remains to-day very much the same as in the time of Plato.

In place, therefore, of adopting a strictly democratic form

of government, which is the ideal of the extreme Communists, the Amana Society has preferred one of an oligarchical nature. The interests of all are entrusted to the wisdom of a few. These act for all. The advantage of this course has been demonstrated, not only in this instance, but in the case of co-operative unions, where the responsibility is generally vested in a few persons who look after the interests of the others.

In the Amana Society rotation in office is not preferred, but annual elections[1] are held, and those who have filled office to satisfaction are generally re-elected. The trustees, to whom is committed the general management of the affairs of the Society, are selected from the men of middle age who understand financial affairs. The elders are chosen from the older members who lead pure lives, and whose services to the Society have been of a faithful and meritorious nature. Thus the most able and the most deserving—those whose fitness is generally acknowledged by the community,—are entrusted with the management of the temporal and moral welfare of all. This conception of Communism and this mode of government may be considered as extremely important elements in the permanency and prosperity of the Community.

To these just-mentioned reasons why the Amana Community has prospered may be added at least two more, and of these the most significant is the system of village life which has been adopted. This preserves a sort of isolation of different groups, while the villages are not far enough apart to interfere in the least with the community-feeling. This segregation into villages has been an important factor in preserving simplicity of life, and in preventing the evils which would probably result from the crowding of all into one town. The Teutonic idea of independent local social organization has asserted itself here, perhaps unconsciously, yet with effect and vigor. The various interests of the villages are overlooked and controlled by the trustees, but the religious and the social

---

1 As to qualification of voters see *Appendix A. Bei-Gesetze.*

independence of each village is preserved. It is indeed a sort of federation—where each small hamlet thinks for itself, but acts in harmony with the religious and social policy of the governing center. To enumerate all the advantages to a community of this semi-independent life would be wearisome, for many of them will occur to every reader.

The use of the German language is another tie which binds the members closely together. Indeed as a common origin, a common religion and a common tongue are three of the most powerful concomitants of national life, so the rule does not fail when the life is not national in any broad sense, but is such as it is in the Amana Community, viz.: that of men and women whose aims, whose beliefs and whose principles are identical.

The seclusion, which to some extent induced the Society to establish itself in Iowa, becomes less and less easy to preserve; the growth of population, the militant character of our civilization and the pressure of competition tend to the destruction of such barriers as must fence in a Community if it preserve its simplicity and antique characteristics. The attractions of a world more cosmopolitan can not but have their legitimate results and lessen by degrees the desire upon the part of the newer generation for the methods of their fathers. As progress is a distinctive principle in our American civilization,—a civilization which is strictly aggressive,—it would be almost too much to hope that the distinctiveness of life which has thus far characterized the Society will be immutable, and remain unaffected by the intense influences from without which require adaptation to themselves in what is unlike them, and, if too strongly opposed, become destructive to what stands in their way.

Among the incidents of their Communistic customs may be mentioned the following:[1]

Women have equal rights in religious affairs. At the elections of officers the voters are all male members who have signed the Constitution, widows, and such female members

---

[1] A statement as to the financial results of their Communism will be found in *Appendix B.*

who are more than thirty years old as are not represented by a male member.[1]

New members are seldom admitted, the growth of the Society being mainly from within.

When a new member joins the Society his property is entrusted to the managers, and he receives credit for it upon their books. Should he at any time desire to leave the Society his money is refunded without interest. When he dies it is inherited by his heirs. Marriage is allowed, but a life of celibacy is considered the ideal one.

Rivalry exists between the members. Each one wishes to excel. At the end of the year persons who have accomplished more than might have been expected receive extra wages and are promoted to places of greater importance. The annual allowance for each person is from $25 to $75. This allowance is only for luxuries of different kinds, and many spend this money in various ways, still it is considered meritorious to place this money also in the general fund to the credit of the person for whom it is held in trust.

Each family has its own house, with all the freedom possible in regard to home affairs. The children are brought up with special religious training. The houses are nearly the same size, so that one family has no better accommodation than another. Around each house there is a garden, which the family can use. These gardens are full of flowers and fruit, which they can sell if they wish. In these they take a great deal of pride, and here they spend much of their leisure time with their families. This spot is the only place that a family can call its own, and here, as in the factories, every man tries to excel his neighbor. These privileges foster that secret pride inherent in every one—the pride of calling something one's own. These rights, although small, help to maintain harmony within the Society. Albert Shaw relates how a quarrel arose in the Icarian Community and nearly shattered it, because the small gardens, in which the members took delight, were destroyed in order to put all on a perfect footing of equality.

---

[1] See *Appendix A. Bei-Gesetze.*

During the summer months nearly three hundred hired laborers are employed. This method of depending on outside labor the members do not approve, for the young may thus be led astray, but they are compelled to rely on other labor than their own. The hired men are treated with as much kindness as if they were members, and the laborers in return appreciate this kindness, for they work for the Society for five dollars per month less than the neighboring farmers pay for the same kind of work.

Hinds believes that they ought to have more in common in order to fully realize the benefits of true Communism. It would undoubtedly be much cheaper to have one "kitchen" in a town of 550 inhabitants, but it would be very inconvenient, especially when we remember, that they eat five times a day. These people look after comfort as well as cheapness, and therefore they have erected sixteen kitchens in Amana, ten in Homestead, and a corresponding number in the other villages. Each village has a laundry, bakery and butcher shop, a butter and cheese factory, and wagons from each of these places make their daily rounds as in the cities.

SCHOOLS.

The members believe in education, and spare neither pains nor money in the training of their children, who, they know, eventually will take their places in the management of the temporal as well as the spiritual affairs of the Society. Education is compulsory, and from seven to fourteen every child must attend school the entire year. Those between fourteen and twenty are compelled to attend during the winter months. The school hours are from eight in the morning until noon. The afternoon is devoted to various kinds of manual training. As there are more than five hundred children under sixteen, the work these willing hands can perform in a few hours is simply enormous. Some are taught gardening, others are instructed in the use of machinery and in the processes of manufacture. That sort of work for which the child shows a natural aptitude is made his life work, i. e., those ready at figures become book-keepers, while others born to command are made foremen of shops and factories. In these schools are taught the rudimentary branches. German and English are taught an hour each, but the conversation in the school hours is carried on in the former language. Mathematics and penmanship must be taught with great care, for ex-Superintendent Mullen said that "he had never visited a school where all could write so well." The schools are public, not parochial, being supported by the township. Amana township, which the Society owns, is divided into independent districts, with a school house in each village. They levy their own school tax, build their own school houses, and employ their own teachers. The teachers are well educated in English. They attend the County Institute, and are examined by the County Superintendent. The wages paid are thirty dollars per month for twelve months, but as the teachers can not keep the money it is turned over to the Society. This amounts then only to a transfer of figures on the books.

THEIR DOMESTIC LIFE.

The members are simple in their habits, and what they call luxuries we look upon as necessaries of life. Their food is wholesome and well prepared. On their tables are found the most excellent bread, the choicest meat, and vegetables of every kind.

Their gardens give evidence of careful cultivation, and are always objects of interest on account of the air of neatness and taste which everywhere prevails in them; the houses are models of cleanliness. There are the massive brown stone houses erected nearly forty years ago; the old frame buildings and the new brick houses, all built on the same plan, and of nearly the same size. There is not a sign of paint on any of the buildings, and this gives to the villages a somber appearance. At Ebenezer they painted their houses, but discovered that it was expensive and did not preserve

the wood long enough to justify the additional cost of a coat
of paint every few years. Neither do they insure their
property, for the same reason, for the premium would amount
to more than the losses by fire. Their factories are not situated closely together, nor are all of them in the same village,
consequently there is less danger in case of a fire than in more
closely settled towns.

The meeting-houses are long and narrow; within, everything is simple,— no pictures, no golden candle-sticks, no
cushioned pews. The long benches are white and seem
almost to have been worn out by frequent scrubbing. At
such a place of worship one sees no woman trying to outshine
her sister, or attract attention by appearing in a bonnet of the
latest style; there are no gossipers at the door waiting until
the first hymn is over, before they enter; but they quietly
take their accustomed places,— the men on the one side, the
women on the other; all observing a reverential demeanor
throughout the service. They are divided into three classes:
1st, the elders and those who are spiritually minded; 2d,
persons of middle age and those less spiritual than the first
class; 3d, children and those who have made but little
progress in religion. According to this division they are
seated; the elders facing the meeting, the children on the
first benches, and the second class behind them. The service
opens with silent prayer when each one communes with the
Creator according to his own needs. It is a solemn silence,
during which no one seems to breathe. This is interrupted
by one of the elders, who announces a hymn which is sung
by the congregation without any instrumental accompaniment.
The entire audience sings, full of enthusiasm, the clear voices
of the women on the one side harmonizing well with the round
full tones of the men. After singing, a chapter is read from
the Bible upon which any one who chooses may comment.
Afterwards follows the reading of some extract from an Inspired
exhortation preserved from the time of the founding of the
Society. Another hymn is sung and the meeting is closed.
The worship is dignified, solemn and deeply impressive; the

hymns, many of them composed by their own members, breathe a pure and Christian spirit, and the manner in which they are sung captivates the ear by reason of its simplicity. On a Sunday quiet broods over the whole village, and one truly realizes that this is a day of rest. Serenity and peace pervade everything.

Their mode of dress is not one assumed or invented by them, but it is the dress of the German peasant of two hundred years ago, with a few changes which convenience, not fashion, have suggested from time to time. At first glance it seems a little strange, but there is a real charm in it, worn as it is by old and young alike. The clean, white bonnet or black cap is becoming to the women, and modest colors, such as black or blue, seem to give the men a dignified bearing. Formerly they made all their own clothing, but do so no longer, as it can be purchased cheaper than they can make it.

Their religion forbids them to turn away anyone suffering from want, thus tramps take advantage of their benevolence. These fellows lurk around in the woods during the day and come to the village after dark, complaining "that they are without work and have had nothing to eat for several days." Compassion is aroused, and they are well cared for in a house set apart for that purpose. In winter it happens frequently that a number of tramps go from village to village, staying a night at each place, and when the circuit has been made, start again on the same round until they are recognized and driven away.

All titles and formal modes of address are viewed with disapprobation, they address one another as "brother" and "sister," they salute one another upon meeting. Though plain in their manner of speech they are courteous and obliging, and as ready to extend a helping hand to an outsider as to one of their own members. Much is said about the gloomy asceticism of Colony life. One living among them will find nothing of this. They are sober and self-possessed, but they have their innocent amusements like others, and those of a lively disposition seem to be admired none the less. When passing their laundries and "kitchens" where the women are working, bursts of innocent laughter mingled with melodious song are to be heard; in their mills and factories the men bending over their work seem pleased and contented, often chanting some well known hymn their mothers taught them. There seems to be a sort of spiritual satisfaction upon their faces, and to a stranger they all look alike, so that it is difficult to distinguish one from another. This may be due to the circumstance that for more than a century they have intermarried within the Society, so that now they are all more or less related; add to this the fact that they think and work in the same manner, sharing each other's joys and sorrows as members of one family, and that they have the same quaintness of apparel, and it is easy to see that there would naturally arise a uniformity of type.

For two hundred years they have existed as a religious Society. For nearly fifty years they have practiced Communism and prospered under it. This is the only Community in the United States which from its foundation until the present time can show a continual increase in membership and value of property. The dying embers of enthusiasm which Christian Metz and Barbara Heinemann stirred up have continued to burn on this side of the ocean. It appears that the doctrines of Spener, Gruber and Rock, like many other doctrines, had to be transplanted into new soil in order to bear the best fruit, From the foundation of the Society the members have always been persons of strong morals and unsullied character, who have clung to their faith with the enthusiasm of true believers, and, persuaded of the truth of their doctrines, have been striving to realize a Heavenly Ideal.

APPENDIX A.[1]

Conſtitution und Bei-Geſetze der Wahren Inſpirations-
Gemeinde, Incorporirt unter dem Namen, „Die
Amana Geſellſchaft zu Amana," im
County und Staat Jowa.

Einleitung.

Nachdem die wahre Inſpirations-Gemeinde im Jahr 1843 und den folgenden Jahren von Deutſchland nach den vereinigten Staaten von Amerika ausgewandert iſt, um die edle bürgerliche und religiöſe Freiheit dieſes Landes zu genießen, und ſich in Eben-Ezer, in der County von Erie im Staat New York, auf der frühern Buffalo Creek Indianer Reſervation, niedergelaſſen hatte, wo dieſelbe ſeitdem unter dem Schutze Gottes in Frieden und Segen beſtanden iſt, ſo wurde im Jahre 1854, nach dem erkannten Willen Gottes von der Gemeinde einmüthig beſchloſ-ſen, das Ebenezer Land zu verkaufen, und eine neue Anſiedlung im Weſten des Landes zu unternehmen.

Es wurde demgemäß im Jahr 1855, und den folgenden Jahren aus dem gemeinſchaftlichen Fond eine Strecke Landes in dem Staat Jowa an-gekauft, und ein Anfang dieſer Ueberſiedlung gemacht, in der Abſicht, ſolche nach und nach auszuführen, wie es die Verhältniſſe erlauben wer-den. Weßhalb wir, die unterſchriebenen Glieder der wahren Inſpira-tions-Gemeinde mit dankbarem Gefühl der Gnade und Güte Gottes, daß wir unter den Geſetzen dieſes freien Staates, unſere Incorporation als eine religiöſe Geſellſchaft erlangen können, uns hiermit unter dem Namen der ,,Amana Geſellſchaft zu Amana.'' im Staate Jowa auf's Neue vereinigten, und die nachfolgende Conſtitu-tion nnd Bei-Geſetze einſtimmig angenommen haben.

---

[1] This is an exact copy of the German constitution, and any grammatical or other errors which may be found appear in the original.

Constitution und Bei-Gesetze.
Artikel 1.

Die Grundfeste auch unserer bürgerlichen Verfassung ist und soll bleiben Gott, der HErr, und der von Ihm aus freier Gnade und Barmherzigkeit in uns gewirkte Glaube, welcher sich gründet, 1) auf das geoffenbarte Wort Gottes im alten und neuen Testament; 2) auf das Zeugniß Jesu durch den Geist der Weissagung; 3) auf den verborgenen Zucht= und Gnaden=Geist des HErrn.

Der Zweck unserer Vereinigung, als eine religiöse Gesellschaft, ist also kein irdischer, noch selbstsüchtiger, sondern der Liebeszweck Gottes in Seiner Gnaden = Berufung an uns, Ihm im Bande der Gemeinschaft von innen und auffen, nach seinen Geboten und Anforderungen in unserm Gewissen, zu dienen, und so das Heil unserer Seelen durch die Erlösungs= Gnade Jesu Christi zu schaffen, mit Verleugnung unserer selbst im Gehor= sam der Wahrheit, und in Erweisung unserer Treue im innern und äußern Dienst der Gemeinde, in der Vermögens=Gnade, die Gott darreicht: Und diese Pflicht zu erfüllen, geloben wir einander Alle gegenseitig an durch die Annahme und Unterschrift dieser gegenwärtigen Constitution und Bei=Gesetze.

Artikel 2.

In diesem von Gott unter uns geknüpften Gemeinschafts = Band ist es unser einmüthiger Wille und Beschluß, daß das hier angekaufte und noch anzukaufende Land ein gemeinschaftliches Gut und Eigenthum sein und bleiben soll, mit allen Anlagen und Verbesserungen darauf, so wie auch mit aller Arbeit, Mühe und Last, wovon jedes Glied sein bescheidenes Theil mit Herzenswilligkeit auf sich nehmen soll. Und da wir in Ge= mäßheit des Staats = Gesetzgebungs = Actes Chapter 131 vom 22. März 1858 unserer Incorporation, als eine religiöse Gesellschaft erlangt haben, so sollen die jetzigen und künftigen Titel zu unserm gemeinschaftlichen Lande an die „Amana Society" als unserm Corporations=Namen, worun= ter wir im Gesetz bekannt sind übertragen und ausgestellt werden.

Artikel 3.

Der Ackerbau und die Viehzucht, in Verbindung mit einigen Manufak= turen und Gewerben, sollen unter dem Segen Gottes die Nahrungs= Zweige dieser Gesellschaft ausmachen. Von dem Ertrag des Landes und der Geschäfte sollen zuvörderst die gemeinschaftlichen Unkosten der Gesell= schaft bestritten werden. Ein allenfallsiger Ueberschuß soll von Zeit zu Zeit zur Verbesserung des gemeinschaftlichen Landes, zur Erbauung und Un=

terhaltung von Schul= und Versammlungshäusern, Druck=anstalten, zur Unterstützung und Verpflegung der alten, kranken und gebrechlichen Glieder der Gesellschaft, zur Anlage eines Geschäfts= und Sicherheits Fondes, und zu wohlthätigen Zwecken im Allgemeinen verwendet werden.

Artikel 4.

Die Leitung und Verwaltung aller Angelegenheiten dieser Gesellschafs soll in 13 Trustees niedergelegt werden, welche von den stimmberechtigten Gliedern derselben, aus der Zahl der Aeltesten jährlich zu erwählen sind. Die Zeit, der Ort und die Weise, wann, wo und wie alle Wahlen für Beamte der Corporation zu halten sind, so wie auch die Wahlfähigkeit der Glieder sollen durch Nebengesetze bestimmt werden, welche von der Gesell= schaft anzunehmen sind. Den so erwählten Trustees ertheilen wir unter= schriebene Glieder hiemit alle Vollmacht, Gerechtsame and Privilegen, welche vom Staatsgesetz den Corporationen verliehen sind, so wie auch alle erforderliche Vollmacht und Gewalt im brüderlichen Einfluß nach unserer Heilsordnung oder in einer Stimmenmehrheit alle Geschäfte und Angelegenheiten dieser Gesetzschaft zu berathen, anzuordnen und zu leiten; neue Glieder unter dieser Constitution anzunehmen, den Gliedern ihre Arbeit und Beschäftigung anzuweisen; die Unterhaltungsgelder derselben zu bestimmen; solche Glieder, welche unordentlich und widerstrebend sind, und auf mehrmalige Ermahnung sich nicht bessern wollen, auszuschließen, auszuweisen, und zu entfernen; die Abrechnungen mit den freiwillig oder gezwungen ausscheidenden Gliedern nach Recht und Billigkeit zu schließen und zu liquidiren, alles active und passive Vermögen der Gesellschaft zu empfangen und zu verwalten; Buch und Rechnung über alles zu führen, zu kaufen und zu verkaufen; Kontracte zu schließen und zu widerrufen; den Ackerbau, die Viehzucht, so wie auch Manufakturen und Gewerbe zu betreiben, Bauten zu errichten, zu verbessern und abzubrechen; Inventa= rien aufzunehmen, Anwälte, Agenten und Aufseher anzustellen, Gelder und Kapitalien zü lehnen, zu verlehnen und sicher anzulegen, so wie auch Güter, Kapitalien, Zinsen, Effekten, Schuldforderungen, Erbschaften, Vermächtnisse und Ausstände aller Art im Namen der Gesellschaft oder irgend eines Gliedes davon zu erheben, einzufordern und zu empfangen; Kaufbriefe, Hypotheken, Schuldscheine, Vollmachten, Quittungen und alle andere Documente und Rechnungen zu empfangen, zu vollziehen und zu überliefern, so wie überhaupt im Namen und Nutzen und Besten dieser Gesellschaft alle nöthige, nützliche, gesetzliche, geeignete, rechtliche und bil= lige Sachen und Handlungen forzunehmen und auszuführen.

Es soll indessen die Pflicht der Trustees sein, über Gegenstände von großer Wichtigkeit und Verantwortung eine extra Sitzung zu halten, in

welcher sie entweder durch einmüthigen Beschluß oder durch Stimmen=
mehrheit zu entscheiden haben, ob die fraglichen Gegenstände allen Ael=
testen nnd sämmtichen stimmfähigen Gesellschafts-Gliedern zur Berath=
ung und Abstimmung vorgelegt werden sollen, oder nicht.

Zu allen Beschlüssen der Trustees, welche den Verkauf des gemeint=
schaftlichen Landes in Town Amana betreffen, ist die Zustimmung von
zwei Drittheilen aller Trustees und Gemeinde-Aeltesten, so wie eine
Mehrheit der stimmfähigen Gesellschafts-Glieder erforderlich. Das Land
außer dem genannten Town gelegen, steht unter der Verwaltung der
Trustees zum Verkauf, Tausch und Verrenten, wie sie solches am besten
und zum Nutzen der Gesellschaft administriren können.

Sollten durch Austritt, Krankheit oder Todt erledigte Stellen in der
Zahl der Trustees entstehen, so können solche Stellen bis zur nächsten
jährlichen Wahl von den Trustees selbst aus der übrigen Aeltesten=Zahl
ergänzt werden.

Die Trustees sollen jährlich aus ihrer Zahl einen Director, einen Vice=
Director und einen Secretair erwählen, und ein Siegel für die Gesell=
schaft als ihr Corporations=Siegel anschaffen. Alle öffentliche und gesetz=
liche Urkunden von der Gesellschaft durch einen Beschluß der Trustees, in
Uebereinstimmung mit dieser Constitution ausgehend, sollen von dem
Director unterzeignet, von dem Secretair gegengezeignet, und mit dem
Corporations=Siegel der Gesellschaft versehen werden.

Im Monat Juni jedes Jahrs soll von den Trustees den stimmbe=
rechtigten Gliedern der Gesellschaft eine vollständige Darstellnng des Ver=
mögens=Zustandes derselben gemacht werden.

Artikel 5.

Jedes Glied dieser Gesellschaft ist verpflichtet, sein mobiles und im=
mobiles Vermöges bei seiner Aufnahme, vor der Unterzeichnung dieser
Constitution, den Trustees für die gemeinschaftliche Kasse ohne Vorbehalt
zu übergeben, und ist dafür zur Gutschrift auf den Büchern der Gesell=
schaft und zu einer Quittung von den dazu bestimmten Trustees berech=
tiget, so wie auch durch das gemeintschaftliche Eigenthum der Gesellschaft
dafür gesichert.

Artikel 6.

Jedes Glied dieser Gesellschaft ist außer der freien Kost und Wohnung,
so wie auch der ihm zugesicherten Verpflegung und Versorgung im Alter,
oder in Krankheit und Gebrechlichkeit, zu einer jährlichen Unterhaltungs=
Summe für sich selbst, Kinder und Angehörige in der Gesellschaft aus der

gemeinschaftlichen Gesellschafts-Kasse berechtiget, und dieses Unterhaltungs-
geld soll jedem Glied, sei es ledig, einzeln oder familienweise, von den
Trustees nach Recht und Billigkeit bestimmt, und von Zeit zu Zeit
geprüft und auf's Neue berichtiget werden, nach einem darüber zu halten-
den Verzeigniß. Und in Anbetracht dieses Genusses der Segnungen im
Gemeinschaftsband verzichten wir unterschriebene Glieder dieser Gesellschaft freiwillig für uns selbst, unsere Kinder, Erben und Administratoren
auf alle andere Ansprüche von Lohn, Zinsen von unsern Einschüssen, Ein-
kommen oder Errungenschaft, so wie überhaupt auf einen vom Ganzen
abgetrennten Antheil an dem gemeinschaftlichen Gut und Eigenthum.

Artikel 7.

Alle Kinder und Minderjährige in der Gesellschaft, stehen nach dem
Tode ihrer Eltern, oder sonstigen Verwandten als Waisen unter der be-
sondern Pflegschaft der Trustees für die Dauer ihrer Minderjährigkeit.
Im Fall solche verstorbene Eltern oder Verwandten ein Guthaben auf den
Büchern der Gesellschaft haben, ohne besondere Willensverfügungen oder
Testamente zu hinterlassen; oder im Fall dieselbe für erhaltene Vor-
schüsse an die Gesellschaft schuldig sind, so treten ihre Kinder mit ihrer
gesetzlichen Volljährlichkeit, was das solcherweise hinterlassene Vermögen,
oder die Verschuldung betrifft, in die Rechte und in die Verbindlichkeit
ihrer verstorbenen Eltern oder Verwandten, als deren natürliche und gesetzliche Erben ein; und das Guthaben oder die Schuld der so verstorbenen Glieder wird dann in den Büchern der Gesellschaft auf solche Erben
nach eines Jeden rechtmässigen Antheil unter der Anordnung der Trustees übertragen. Solche Hinterlassenschaften von Gesellschafts-Gliedern,
welche ohne Willensverfügung und Testament, und ohne gesetzliche Erben
zu hinterlassen versterben, sollen der Gesellschaft selbst anheimfallen.

Artikel 8.

Glieder, welche aus der Gesellschaft freiwillig austreten oder ausgewiesen
werden, sind zum Zurück-Empfang ihrer Einlagen in die gemeinschaftliche
Kasse berechtigt, und, von der Zeit der Abrechnung mit ihnen an gerechnet,
zu einer Zinsenvergütung, welche fünf Procent per Jahr nicht übersteigen,
und von den Trustees bestimmt werden soll, für solche gemachte Einlagen,
bis zu deren Zurückzahlung, aber zu keiner andern Vergütung für die der
Gesellschaft während ihrer Gliederschaft geleistete Dienste, als solche,
welche ihnen von den Trustees derselben bei der Abrechnung mit ihnen
freiwillig zuerkannt werden mag. Und indessen die Gesellschaft in den
Stand zu setzen, solche Rückzahlungen von Einschüssen austretender Glie-

der, so wie auch etwaige Zahlungen von Vermächtnissen und Erbschaften, welche von Personen außer der Gesellschaft beansprucht werden können, ohne Schaden und Bedrückung leisten zu können, so sind wir dahin überein gekommen, daß solche Zahlungen auf folgenden Weise geleistet werden sollen, nämlich, von allen Summen bis zu 500 Dollars ein Viertheil bei der Abrechnung oder Feststellung der Forderung, und der Rest innerhalb vier Monaten; von allen Summen von über $500 bis $20,000 und darüber, von $200 bis $600 bei der Abrechnung, und der Rest in je 3, 4, 6, 9, 12, 15, 18 und 21 gleichen viermonatlichen Terminen im Verhältniß zu dem Betrag der zu zahlenden Summen. Unser Sinn dabei ist, Niemand ohne Noth das Seine vorzuenthalten, aber doch auch für alle Fälle die Gesellschaft gegen Noth und Verlegenheit zu schützen, weshalb den Trustees zustehen soll nach Zeit und Umständen hierin zu handeln, und sich mit den betreffenden Creditoren in solchen Fällen nach Recht und Billigkeit zu verständigen.

Artikel 9.

Verbesserungen und Zusätze zu dieser Constitution können jederzeit von den Gliedern der Gesellschaft den Trustees zur Prüfung und Berathung vorgeschlagen werden, erfordern aber zur Annahme, als ein Theil dieser Constitution, die Zustimmung von zwei Drittheilen der sämmtlichen Trustees, so wie auch der übrigen Gemeinde-Aeltesten, und eine Mehrheit der stimmfähigen Glieder.

Artikel 10.

Diese Constitution soll am ersten Januar A. D. 1860 in Kraft treten, und von allen volljährigen Glieder dieser Gesellschaft beiderlei Geschlechts unterschrieben werden in einem besonders dazu bestimmten und von den Trustees aufzubewahrenden Buche. Ein Exemplar davon soll jedem stimmfähigen Glied auf Verlangen zur Einsicht behändigt werden.

Gethan in öffentlicher Versammlung, urkundlich unser Unterschriften.

Amana, in der County und im Staat Jowa, im Monat December 1859.

Bei-Gesetze.
Die Wahl betreffend.

Die Wahl soll jährlich am ersten Dienstag im Monat December gehalten werden.

Alle männliche Glieder, die die Constitution unterschrieben haben, so wie auch Wittwen und solche weibliche Glieder, die über dreißig Jahre alt find, und nicht durch ein männliches Glied repräsentirt find, sollen zur Wahl berechtigt sein.

Die Wähler sollen an dem gesagten Wahltag durch Stimmzettel 13 Trustees wählen, für die Zeit eines Jahrs, anfangend am ersten Januar jeden Jahrs.

Die 13 Trustees sollen am 2. Dienstag im Monat December einen Director, einen Vice=Director und einen Secretair aus ihrer Anzahl er= wählen, ebenfalls durch Stimmzettel.

Die Wahl soll in dem Schul= und Versammlungshaus des ersten Schulsubdistrikts des Amana Townships gehalten werden. Irgend eine Veränderumg des Wahlorts oder der Zeit soll den Wählern 14 Tag vor der Wahl mitgetheilt werden.

Die Township Trustees und Clerk sollen die Leiter der Wahl sein.

APPENDIX A.[1]

CONSTITUTION AND BY-LAWS OF THE COMMUNITY OF TRUE INSPIRATION, INCORPORATED UNDER THE NAME OF "THE AMANA SOCIETY," IN THE TOWN OF AMANA IN THE COUNTY AND STATE OF IOWA.

PREAMBLE.

Whereas the Community of True Inspiration hath in the year 1843, and the following years emigrated from Germany into the United States of America, for the sake of enjoying the noble civil and religious liberty of this country, and hath settled at Eben-Ezer, in the County of Erie and State of New York, on the Buffalo Creek Indian Reservation, where they have since existed, under the protection of God, in peace and prosperity; and whereas the said Community in the year 1854, according to the known will of God, resolved unanimously, to sell the Eben-Ezer lands, and to undertake a new settlement in the western country, and hath consequently in the year 1855 and the years following, purchased a tract of

---

[1] The translation of the German text of the Constitution is the authorized one in use in the Community.

land in the State of Iowa, and paid for the same out of the
funds of the Community; and whereas since a beginning hath
been made of this new settlement, with the purpose to continue and accomplish such resettlement by degrees, as the
times and circumstances will permit.

Now therefore, we the undersigned members of the Community of True Inspiration, feeling thankful for the grace and
beneficence of God, to be privileged under the liberal laws
of this state to an incorporation as a religious Society, do
hereby associate ourselves anew under the corporate name of
"THE AMANA SOCIETY,"
in the Town of Amana, and have adopted and do herewith
adopt the following Constitution and By-Laws.

CONSTITUTION AND BY-LAWS.

ARTICLE I.

The foundation of our civil organization is and shall remain
forever God, the Lord, and the faith, which He worked in
us according to His free grace and mercy, and which is
founded upon (1) the word of God as revealed in the old
and new testament; (2) the testimony of Jesus through
the spirit of prophecy; (3) the hidden spirit of grace and
chastisement.

The purpose of our association as a religious Society is
therefore no worldly or selfish one, but the purpose of the love
of God in His vocation of grace received by us, to serve Him
in the inward and outward bond of union, according to His
laws and His requirements in our own consciences, and thus
to work out the salvation of our souls, through the redeeming
grace of Jesus Christ, in self-denial, in the obedience of our
faith and in the demonstration of our faithfulness in the inward
and outward service of the Community by the power of
grace, which God presents us with.

And to fulfill this duty we do hereby covenant and promise
collectively and each to the other by the acceptance and signing of this present constitution.

ARTICLE II.

In this bond of union tied by God amongst ourselves, it is our unanimous will and resolution, that the land purchased here and that may hereafter be purchased, shall be and remain a common estate and property, with all improvements thereupon and all appurtenances thereto, as also with all the labor, cares, troubles and burdens, of which each member shall bear his allotted share with a willing heart.

And having obtained in pursuance of the act of the legislature of this state, Chapter 131, passed March 28th, 1858, an incorporation as a religious Society, it is hereby agreed on that the present and future titles of our common lands shall be conveyed to and vested in "the Amana Society" in the Town of Amana, as our corporate name by which we are known in law.

ARTICLE III.

Agriculture and the raising of cattle and other domestic animals, in connection with some manufactures and trades shall under the blessing of God form the means of sustenance for this Society. Out of the income of the land and the other branches of industry the common expenses of the Society shall be defrayed.

The surplus, if any, shall from time to time be applied to the improvement of the common estate of the Society, to the building and maintaining of meeting and school houses, printing establishments, to the support and care of the old, sick and infirm members of the Society, to the founding of a business and safety fund, and to benevolent purposes in general.

ARTICLE IV.

The control and management of all the affairs of this Society shall be vested in a board of Trustees consisting of thirteen members, to be annually elected out of the number of elders in the Community, by the members of the Society entitled to vote. The time, place and manner of holding all elections for officers in this corporation and the qualifi-

majority, in regard to such credits or debts, enter into the rights and into the liabilities of their deceased parents and relations, as their natural and lawful heirs, and the credits or debts of members so deceased shall then be transferred on the books of the Society to such heirs, according to the proper share of each, under the direction of the trustees. Such personal estates or credits as may be left by members, dying in the Society, without having made any will or testament for the disposition of the same, and without leaving any lawful heirs, shall revert to and vest in said corporation.

ARTICLE VIII.

Such members as may recede from the Society, either by their own choice or by expulsion, shall be entitled to receive back the moneys paid into the common fund, and to interest thereon at the rate not exceeding five per cent. per annum, from the time of the adjustment of their accounts until the repayment of their credits, which rate is to be fixed by the board of trustees.

Such receding members shall however not be entitled to any other allowance for any services rendered to the Society during their membership, but to such, as may be granted them by the board of trustees, on the settlement of their accounts, as a gratuity and not as a legal claim.

To enable however the Society to make such repayments to receding members, as also eventual payments of legacies and inheritances of members deceased in the Society, to relations or heirs thereto entitled beyond the Society, without loss and oppression, it has been agreed on between ourselves, that such payments shall be made in the following manner, viz: of all sums up to $500, one-fourth part on the adjustment of the claim, and the remainder within four months thereafter; of all sums over $500 up to $20,000, and over, the sum of from $200 to $600 at the time of settlement, and the remainder in three, four, six, nine, twelve, fifteen, eighteen and twenty-one equal four-monthly installments, in proportion to the amounts to be paid.

fications of voters shall be regulated by by-laws to be adopted by the Community.

In the trustees, so elected, we the undersigned members do hereby vest all the powers, rights of action and privileges granted to corporations by the laws of this state, and also all requisite power and authority to arrange, control and manage, in brotherly concurrence according to our order of grace, or by a majority of votes, all the affairs and concerns of this corporation whatsoever; to receive new members under this constitution; to assign to the members their work, labor and employment; to fix the amounts of the yearly allowances for the support of the members; to exclude, order away and remove such members who are unruly and resisting, and who will not mend themselves after repeated admonition; to settle and liquidate the accounts of those members withdrawing from the Society, either by their own choice or by expulsion; to receive and to administrate all the active and passive capital stock and personal estate of the Society; to keep books and accounts of every thing; to buy and to sell; to make, fulfill and revoke contracts, to carry on agriculture, the rearing of cattle, manufactures, mills and trades of any kind, to erect buildings, to improve and take down the same; to make inventories; to appoint attorneys, agents and managers; to borrow, lend and safely invest funds and moneys; also in the corporate name of the Society, or in the name of the trustees, or of any member thereof to ask, demand, levy, recover and receive all kinds of goods, moneys, principal and interest, effects, debts, demands, inheritances and legacies, wheresoever and whatsoever; to receive, execute and deliver all deeds, mortgages, notes, bonds, power of attorney, receipts, discharges, and all other documents and accounts whatsoever; and to do, transact and carry out all needful, beneficial, legal, proper, just and equitable acts, matters and things in general of all and every kind whatsoever, all for and in the name, behalf and benefit of this corporation.

In the event however of matters of great importance and responsibility it shall be the duty of the trustees to hold special meetings and to decide therein either by unanimous concurrence or by a majority of votes whether or not such matters shall be submitted for counsel and decision by vote to all the elders of the Community and to the members entitled to vote.

All resolutions of the board of trustees relating to the sale of the Society's lands situate within the Town of Amana require the consent of two-thirds of all the trustees and of two-thirds of all the elders in the Community, as also the consent of a majority of the members entitled to vote.

The lands now owned by the Society lying beyond the Town of Amana shall be under the administration of the trustees with power to sell, exchange or rent the same, as they shall find best in the interest of the Society.

Vacancies in the board of trustees occasioned by withdrawal, sickness or death of any of its members, may be filled for the intervening time until the next annual election by the remaining trustees themselves, out of the number of the elders in the Community, not being members elected to the board.

In the month of June in each year the trustees shall exhibit to the voting members of the Society a full statement of the real and personal estate of the Society.

The trustees shall annually elect out of their number one Director, one vice-director and one secretary, and shall procure a seal, which shall be the corporate seal of the Society.

All public and legal documents and instruments emanating from the Society by a resolution of the trustees, in conformity with this constitution, shall be signed by the director, countersigned by the secretary, and the corporate seal of the Society affixed thereto.

On the application of any three members of the board of trustees it shall be the duty of the director to call an extra or special meeting of said board.

Article V.

Every member of this Society is in duty bound to hand over his or her personal and real property to the trustees

for the common fund, at the time of his or her acceptance as a member, and before the signing of this constitution.

For such payments into the common fund each member is entitled to the credit thereof in the books of the Society and to a receipt signed by the director and secretary of the board of trustees, and is moreover secured for such payments by the pledge of the common property of the Society.

Article VI.

Every member of this Society is, besides the free boa and dwelling, and the support and care secured to him in old age, sickness and infirmity, further entitled out of common fund to an annual sum of maintenance for him herself, children and relations in the Society; and th annual allowances shall be fixed by the trustees for e member single or in families, according to justice and eq and shall be from time to time revised and fixed anew.

And we, the undersigned members of this corporati consideration of the enjoyment of these blessings in the of our Communion, do hereby release, grant and quit- to the said corporation, for ourselves, our children, heir administrators all claims for wages and interest of the c paid into the common fund, also all claims of any part income and profits, and of any share in the estate and erty of the Society separate from the whole and co stock.

Article VII.

All children and minors in the Society, after th of their parents or relations, shall as orphans be the special guardianship of the trustees of the during the time of their minority. In case of such pa relations deceased having a credit on the books of the without their leaving a will or testament for the disp the same; or in case such parents or relations are in the Society for advances made them, then the ch minors of such parents and relations shall at the tim

Our purpose is not to withhold from any one his due without necessity, but also to secure the Society in all cases against distress and trouble; the authority shall therefore be left with our trustees to act herein according to the times and circumstances, and to effect a compromise with the claimants in question according to justice and equity.

ARTICLE IX.

Amendments to this constitution may at any time be proposed by any member of this Society to the board of trustees for counsel and examination. Any amendments however to be received and accepted as a part of the present constitution, require the consent of two-thirds of the board of trustees, of two-thirds of the remaining elders, and of a majority of the members entitled to vote.

ARTICLE X.

This constitution shall take effect on the first of January, 1860, and shall be signed by all members of lawful age, male and female, in a separate book to be appropriated hereto and to be left in the safe keeping of the board of trustees. A copy of this constitution shall upon request be handed to any voting member of the Society for perusal and reference.

Done in public meeting.

Witness our signatures.

Amana, in the County and State of Iowa, in the month of December, A. D. 1859.

APPENDIX B.[1]

ASSESSED VALUATION OF ALL PROPERTY OWNED BY THE AMANA SOCIETY, IN IOWA COUNTY, FOR THE YEAR 1890.[2]

	Number.	Value.
Acres, - - - - - -	23,211$\frac{68}{100}$	$277,440
Horses, - - - - -	273	8,080
Cattle, - - - - - -	1,685	11,456
Sheep, - - - - -	3,035	4,570
Swine, - - - - - -	825	619
Vehicles, - - - - -	302	2,425
Merchandise, - - - -		48,365
Capital Employed in Manufactures,		46,375
Moneys and Credits, - - -		14,080
Farming and Mechanics' Tools, Etc.,		975
Other Taxable Property, - -		3,068

Grand Total of all Property, - - - $417,453

Assessment Amana Society, 1890, -	$417,453.00
Number of Members, 1890, - -	1666
Average Assessment, 1890, - -	$250.57+

In order that the average assessment of the members of the Amana Society may be compared (1) with the average assessment of the inhabitants of Iowa, (2) with that of the inhabitants of Iowa county, the following figures taken from the Auditors' reports are appended.

STATE OF IOWA, 1890.

Total Assessment of Iowa, 1890, -	$523,198,984.00
Population of Iowa, 1890, - -	1,911,896
State Assessment per capita, 1890, -	$273.65+

[1] Assessments based on 33⅓ per cent of actual value.
[2] These figures are a transcript from the Auditors' books.

IOWA COUNTY, 1890.

Total Assessment Iowa County, 1890,	$4,950,830.00
Total Population Iowa County, 1890,	18,261
Assessment in Iowa County per capita 1890 - - - - -	$271.11+

IOWA COUNTY, EXCLUSIVE OF AMANA SOCIETY, 1890.

Assessed value Iowa County, 1890, -	$4,950,830.00
Assessed value Amana Society, 1890,	$417,453.00
Assessed value Iowa County, less valuation Amana Society, 1890, -	$4,533,377.00
Population Iowa County, 1890, -	18,261
Population Amana Society, 1890, -	1,666
Population Iowa County, less Amana Society, 1890, - - -	16,595
Assessment Iowa County per capita, less Amana Society, 1890, -	$273.44+

SUMMARY.

Assessment in State per capita, 1890, - -	$273.65
Assessment in Iowa County per capita, 1890,	271.11
Assessment in Iowa County per capita, leaving out Amana Society, 1890, - - -	273.44+
Assessment Amana Society per capita, 1890,	250.57+

Two inferences may be drawn from the above figures; first, that the assessment in the case of the Amana Society is not high enough; second, that communistic does not pay as well as uncommunistic labor. The authors of this monograph believe that the latter is the true reason for the discrepancy between the averages, and, that on the whole, communistic enterprises fall behind in productiveness.

This last statement may however be modified by the facts that at the present time there are perhaps more than the average number of unproductive members, i. e., those incapacitated for labor by age; and that the number of children, who are to a great extent unproductive, approaches five hundred. All these have to be supported by the Society without much return. It is not unlikely that the unproductive members are in excess, at the present time, of the average. If this be the case the assessment of 1890 would hardly be a fair test of the efficiency of communistic labor.

APPENDIX C.

AUTHORITIES CONSULTED IN THE PREPARATION OF THIS ARTICLE.

(The first list may be considered original sources, as the books referred to are found only in the records and libraries of the Society.)

The Constitution of the Society.

Scheuner, Gottlieb—Inspirations-Historie, 2 vols., 1884, (vol. III in preparation.)

Published by the Society Each Year—Jahrbücher der Wahren-Inspirations-Gemeinde, oder Bezeugungen von dem Geiste des Herrn.

Erster Beitrag zur Fortsetzung der Wahren-Inspirations-Gemeinschaft.

Die XXXVI Sammlung, (Dieses ist die Zweite Fortsetzung von Bruder Johann Friedrich Rock's Reisen und Religiösen Besuchen im Jahr 1714, etc.) 1785.

Metz, Christian— Historische Beschreibungen der Wahren-Inspirations-Gemeinschaft, wie sie bestanden und sich fortgepflanzt hat, und was von den wichtigsten Ereignissen noch ausgefunden werden kann, besonders wie sie in den Jahren 1817 und 1818 durch den Geist Gottes in neuen Werkzeugen aufgeweckt worden und was seit der Zeit in und mit dieser Gemeinde und deren herzugekommenen Gliedern Wichtiges vorgefallen.

Petersen, Johann W.—Werke.

Kämpf, Johann Philip—Die Unchristlichen Gebräuche von den Kindern Christi unter den Leuten.

Metz, Christian — Sammlung Zwanzig (Jahrbücher, 1817–1845.)

Metz, Christian—Historie der Wahren-Inspirations-Gemeinde. 2d part.

Rock, Johann Fr.— Reise Beschreibungen.

Eine Kurze Beschreibung von Barbara Heinemann wie dieselbe Gottlieb Scheuner von ihr erzählt wurde in ihrem 73ten Lebensjahr.

Lebensgeschichte von Kämpf, Löwe, Gruber und Gleim, 1875.

THE FOLLOWING BOOKS CONTAIN THE CREED OF THE SOCIETY.

Die Schule der Weisheit, als das Hoch Deutsche A, B, C.

Catechitischer Unterricht von der Lehre des Heils.   1879.

Der Kleine Kempis oder Kurze Sprüche und Gebete. (Selections from the works of Thomas à Kempis.)   1856.

Seelen-Schatz der Gott-Begierigen, etc.   1851.

Stimmen aus Zion, zum Lobe des Allmächtigen im Geist gesungen, von Dr. Johann W. Petersen.

Davidisches Psalter-Spiel der Kinder Zions. (A collection of hymns.)   1871.

Das Liebes- und Gedächtniszmahl des Leidens und Sterbens unsers Herrn und Heilandes Jesu Christi.   1859.

Exegetische Reimen-Probe über die Letzte Rede unsers Herrn Jesu Christi an Seine Wahrhaftigen Jünger. E. L. Gruber, 1860.

OTHER WORKS CONSULTED.

Arnoldi—History of Pietism.
Dorner—Church History.
Vaughan, R.—Hours with Mystics.
Moehler, J. A.—Symbolism.
Hurst—Rationalism.
Schaff—Creeds of Christianity.
Giessler—Church History.

Wylie, J. A.—History of Protestantism.

Hosbach, W.—Spener and his Time.

Clark, J. F.—Events and Epochs in Religious History.

Molinos—Guide to Contemplation.

Gerhard, John—Exegetical Explanation of Particular Passages.

Arndt, Johann—True Christianity.

Autobiography of Madam Guyon.

Works and Life of Thomas à Kempis.

Life of Boehme.

Works of Count Zinsendorf.

Articles on the Moravian Brothers.

Hinds, W. A.—American Communism. 1878.

Wolsey—Communism and Socialism. 1880.

Godwin, P.—The Ebenezer Community, published in People's Journal, vol. IV, p. 218.

Owen, Robert D.—The Moral World.

Morse—Communistic Societies.

Rae, John—Contemporary Socialism.

Noyes, J. H.—History of American Socialism.

Shaw, Albert—Icaria.

MID-AMERICAN FRONTIER

An Arno Press Collection

Andreas, A[lfred] T[heodore]. **History of Chicago.** 3 volumes. 1884-1886

Andrews, C[hristopher] C[olumbus]. **Minnesota and Dacotah.** 1857

Atwater, Caleb. **Remarks Made on a Tour to Prairie du Chien:** Thence to Washington City, in 1829. 1831

Beck, Lewis C[aleb]. **A Gazetteer of the States of Illinois and Missouri.** 1823

Beckwith, Hiram W[illiams]. **The Illinois and Indiana Indians.** 1884

Blois, John T. **Gazetteer of the State of Michigan, in Three Parts.** 1838

Brown, Jesse and A. M. Willard. **The Black Hills Trails.** 1924

Brunson, Alfred. **A Western Pioneer: Or, Incidents of the Life and Times of Rev. Alfred Brunson.** 2 volumes in one. 1872

Burnet, Jacob. **Notes on the Early Settlement of the North-Western Territory.** 1847

Cass, Lewis. **Considerations on the Present State of the Indians, and their Removal to the West of the Mississippi.** 1828

Coggeshall, William T[urner]. **The Poets and Poetry of the West.** 1860

Darby, John F[letcher]. **Personal Recollections of Many Prominent People Whom I Have Known.** 1880

Eastman, Mary. **Dahcotah:** Or, Life and Legends of the Sioux Around Fort Snelling. 1849

Ebbutt, Percy G. **Emigrant Life in Kansas.** 1886

Edwards, Ninian W[irt]. **History of Illinois, From 1778 to 1833:** And Life and Times of Ninian Edwards. 1870

Ellsworth, Henry William. **Valley of the Upper Wabash, Indiana.** 1838

Esarey, Logan, ed. **Messages and Letters of William Henry Harrison.** 2 volumes. 1922

Flower, George. **The Errors of Emigrants.** [1841]

Hall, Baynard Rush (Robert Carlton, pseud.). **The New Purchase:** Or Seven and a Half Years in the Far West. 2 volumes in one. 1843

Haynes, Fred[erick] Emory. **James Baird Weaver.** 1919

Heilbron, Bertha L., ed. **With Pen and Pencil on the Frontier in 1851:** The Diary and Sketches of Frank Blackwell Mayer. 1932

Hinsdale, B[urke] A[aron]. **The Old Northwest:** The Beginnings of Our Colonial System. [1899]

Johnson, Harrison. **Johnson's History of Nebraska.** 1880

Lapham, I[ncrease] A[llen]. **Wisconsin: Its Geography and Topography,** History, Geology, and Mineralogy. 1846

Mansfield, Edward D. **Memoirs of the Life and Services of Daniel Drake.** 1855

Marshall, Thomas Maitland, ed. **The Life and Papers of Frederick Bates.** 2 volumes in one. 1926

McConnel, J[ohn] L[udlum.] **Western Characters: Or, Types of Border** Life in the Western States. 1853

Miller, Benjamin S. **Ranch Life in Southern Kansas and the Indian Territory.** 1896

Neill, Edward Duffield. **The History of Minnesota.** 1858

Parker, Nathan H[owe]. **The Minnesota Handbook, For 1856-7.** 1857

Peck, J[ohn] M[ason]. **A Guide for Emigrants.** 1831

Pelzer, Louis. **Marches of the Dragoons in the Mississippi Valley.** 1917

Perkins, William Rufus and Barthinius L. Wick. **History of the Amana Society.** 1891

Rister, Carl Coke. **Land Hunger:** David L. Payne and the Oklahoma Boomers. 1942

Schoolcraft, Henry R[owe]. **Personal Memoirs of a Residence of Thirty Years With the Indian Tribes on the American Frontiers.** 1851

Smalley, Eugene V. **History of the Northern Pacific Railroad.** 1883

[Smith, William Rudolph]. **Observations on the Wisconsin Territory.** 1838

Steele, [Eliza R.] **A Summer Journey in the West.** 1841

Streeter, Floyd Benjamin. **The Kaw:** The Heart of a Nation. 1941

[Switzler, William F.] **Switzler's Illustrated History of Missouri,** From 1541 to 1877. 1879

Tallent, Annie D. **The Black Hills.** 1899

Thwaites, Reuben Gold. **On the Storied Ohio.** 1903

Todd, Charles S[tewart] and Benjamin Drake. **Sketches of the Civil and Military Services of William Henry Harrison.** 1840

Wetmore, Alphonso, compiler. **Gazetteer of the State of Missouri.** 1837

Wilder, D[aniel] W[ebster]. **The Annals of Kansas.** 1886

Woollen, William Wesley. **Biographical and Historical Sketches of Early Indiana.** 1883

Wright, Robert M[arr]. **Dodge City.** 1913